Shake Jiggle & Roll

Peter Rogers & John E Turner

Greg Dwyer, Sue Rogers & Maz Turner

To the Wonderful Peter & Leo.

Peter Rogers

John. E. Turner.

All authors' profits go to The Cure Parkinson's Trust

A Bright Pen Book
© Text: Peter Rogers & John E Turner 2012
© Design & Illustrations: Peter Rogers 2012
© Photographs: Greg Dwyer, John E Turner,
    Peter Rogers, Mike Peel, Tom Phillips 2012

All rights reserved. No part of this publication
may be reproduced, stored in a retrieval system,
or transmitted in any form or by any means,
electronic, mechanical, photocopy, recording or
otherwise, without prior written permission of
the copyright owner. Nor can it be circulated in
any form of binding or cover other than that in
which it is published and without similar condition
including this condition being imposed on a
subsequent purchaser.

British Library Cataloguing in Publication Data.
A catalogue record for this book is available from
the British Library.

ISBN 978-0-7552-1545-4

Every reasonable attempt has been made by
the authors to correctly acknowledge the original
sources of all quotes used.

Authors OnLine Ltd
19 The Cinques, Gamlingay, Sandy,
Bedfordshire SG19 3NU, England.

Shake Jogle & Roll

Two accounts of one twenty-nine day
854 mile run from John O'Groats to Land's End
in aid of The Cure Parkinson's Trust

'I hitch-hiked round Ireland with a fridge. John and Peter ran the length of Britain in under a month. The similarities are there for all to see, except for the fact that I was driven everywhere in cars, and then strolling into pubs, and they ran everywhere and then collapsed into exhausted heaps at the end of every day. All the more reason for supporting them - not least because their endeavour was all about finding a cure for Parkinson's. And, fridge or not, that's the coolest thing of all.'

Tony Hawks

The Cure Parkinson's Trust
Charity Number : 1111816

Contents

Peter's story: One step at a time — 5
Foreword — 8
Preparing the way — 10
The main characters — 13
My personal motivation — 14
The Jogle — 16
Training for the big one — 82
Route and schedule — 86
Actual statistics — 87
Post run reflections — 88
Reflections of the wife — 91
Acknowledgements — 94

Greg's Story: The view from the driver's seat — 99
Introduction — 100
The journey begins — 102

John's Story: Trolling Down Hill — 107
Who am I? — 108
Foreword 1 — 116
Foreword 2 — 119
The Jogle — 121
Snippets — 154
Who said staying at home was easy? — 159

Appendices — 160
Some helpful reading — 160
A few useful Apps — 162
Running kit — 164
Medical and foot care kit — 165
Our take on nutrition — 166
Maps and navigation — 168
Our major sponsors — 169

For Mum - my rock and inspiration

One step at a time

When I discovered running, I discovered time, distance and space. Living on an island, I guess it was only really a matter of time until I pushed it to the limit...

Peter's story

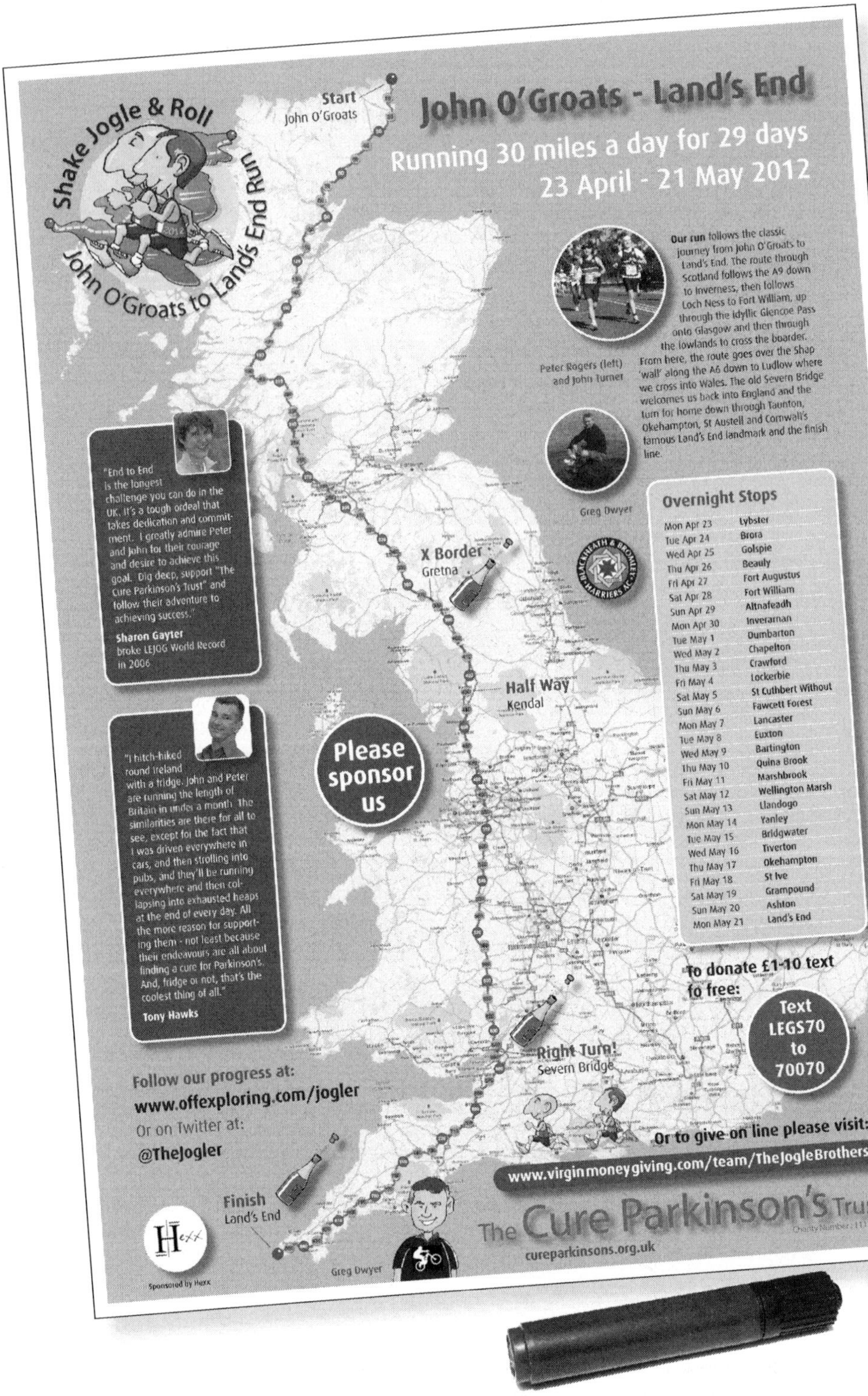

John O'Groats - Land's End
Running 30 miles a day for 29 days
23 April - 21 May 2012
Shake Jogle & Roll
John O'Groats to Land's End Run
Start
John O'Groats
Our run follows the classic journey from John O'Groats to Land's End. The route through Scotland follows the A9 down to Inverness, then follows Loch Ness to Fort William, up through the idyllic Glencoe Pass onto Glasgow and then through the lowlands to cross the boarder. From here, the route goes over the Shap 'wall' along the A6 down to Ludlow where we cross into Wales. The old Severn Bridge welcomes us back into England and the turn for home down through Taunton, Okehampton, St Austell and Cornwall's famous Land's End landmark and the finish line.
Peter Rogers (left) and John Turner
Greg Dwyer
"End to End is the longest challenge you can do in the UK. It's a tough ordeal that takes dedication and commitment. I greatly admire Peter and John for their courage and desire to achieve this goal. Dig deep, support "The Cure Parkinson's Trust" and follow their adventure to achieving success."
Sharon Gayter
broke LEJOG World Record in 2006
X Border
Gretna
Half Way
Kendal
Please sponsor us
"I hitch-hiked round Ireland with a fridge. John and Peter are running the length of Britain in under a month. The similarities are there for all to see, except for the fact that I was driven everywhere in cars, and then strolling into pubs, and they'll be running everywhere and then collapsing into exhausted heaps at the end of every day. All the more reason for supporting them - not least because their endeavours are all about finding a cure for Parkinson's. And, fridge or not, that's the coolest thing of all."
Tony Hawks
Overnight Stops
Mon Apr 23 Lybster
Tue Apr 24 Brora
Wed Apr 25 Golspie
Thu Apr 26 Beauly
Fri Apr 27 Fort Augustus
Sat Apr 28 Fort William
Sun Apr 29 Altnafeadh
Mon Apr 30 Inverarnan
Tue May 1 Dumbarton
Wed May 2 Chapelton
Thu May 3 Crawford
Fri May 4 Lockerbie
Sat May 5 St Cuthbert Without
Sun May 6 Fawcett Forest
Mon May 7 Lancaster
Tue May 8 Euxton
Wed May 9 Bartington
Thu May 10 Quina Brook
Fri May 11 Marshbrook
Sat May 12 Wellington Marsh
Sun May 13 Llandogo
Mon May 14 Yanley
Tue May 15 Bridgwater
Wed May 16 Tiverton
Thu May 17 Okehampton
Fri May 18 St Ive
Sat May 19 Grampound
Sun May 20 Ashton
Mon May 21 Land's End
To donate £1-10 text for free:
Text LEGS70 to 70070
Right Turn!
Severn Bridge
Follow our progress at:
www.offexploring.com/jogler
Or on Twitter at:
@TheJogler
Or to give on line please visit:
www.virginmoneygiving.com/team/TheJogleBrothers
Finish
Land's End
The Cure Parkinson's Trust
cureparkinsons.org.uk
Greg Dwyer
Sponsored by Hexx

Dear Peter and John

'I think it's wonderful when a plan comes together. You have done the planning and organising and obviously the training and this looks like a well oiled machine that will go the distance. You have been realistic, set a goal that is challenging and will work you hard, but the achievement will be every bit as big as mine was. I set a goal and achieved it and that is exactly what you are doing. Be proud, keep fit and go and enjoy the experience. There will be lows but you will look back on this adventure for the rest of your lives when you achieve it.

Good luck you two - I am sure you will go well with each other for support. You never know I may just pop up on your route somewhere!'

Sharon Gayter

Sharon Gayter
Broke the LEJOG World Record in 2006

Opposite: We plan to mark off each 30 mile section on one of our posters every night

Foreword (Forward!)

> 'Don't bother just to be better than your contemporaries or predecessors. Try to be better than yourself.'
>
> **William Faulkner**

I don't like speed. Speed is not my thing. I have never felt very comfortable going fast. And I'm certainly never likely to win a race, unless the competition should ever fail to turn up. Distance is what I really enjoy.

I enjoy the challenge of the journey when you run long distances. When running alone I enjoy exploring the place in my head that only my running shoes can take me, and when running with others, I enjoy the camaraderie, the friendship and the conversation.

I love the simplicity of running. It doesn't rely on expensive equipment. All I have to do is pull on a pair of shoes and head out the door. I love the purity of the sport. It's me against the road. I try to keep it as simple and as enjoyable as possible.

When I discovered running I discovered the freedom of time, distance and space. Living on an island, I guess it was only really a matter of time until I pushed it to the limit (so thanks mum!). I have always been fascinated to know just how far I can go. After seventeen years of asking the question I've yet to discover the answer. The next twenty-nine days might finally reveal all.

I can't tell you how delighted I was when my good friend John agreed to join me on the journey. JT and I have been long running friends for many years - 'Joined at the hip' some might say, 'brothers in legs' would be our response. We have run and raced many thousands of miles together. Seeds of an End to End or Trans-Continental run have often been sown during our long training runs, so I guess it's little surprise that one of those seeds has finally taken root and sprung to life. Not many 61, almost 62, year olds would consider taking up such a challenge. By just standing at the start he has my utmost respect and admiration. There is, quite simply, no one else I would rather make this journey of discovery with.

I am equally delighted that another good friend, Greg Dwyer, an experienced multi day eventer, readily volunteered, at his own expense, to fly halfway around the world to enable us to fulfil our dream. I am in absolutely no doubt that without his valuable support it would have been impossible.

The biggest surprise of the whole venture, for me, was the extraordinary level of interest and support generated by the daily blog. And even more surprising, the numerous requests to either continue or publish it upon our return! It's almost impossible to believe that so many people had nothing better to do for a whole month! So by popular demand, here it is, the expanded, unabridged version with a selection of your daily comments.

I invite you now to sit back, relax and re-live (or discover anew) the spectacle of two oddballs and a crazy Australian - hobble, wobble and 'jogle' their way down the country for your delectation and delight. Let the games begin....

Friesland, July 2012

Running the 90k Comrades ultra marathon with JT in South Africa, 2005

Preparing the way

'If you fail to prepare, prepare to fail.'

Steve Prefontaine

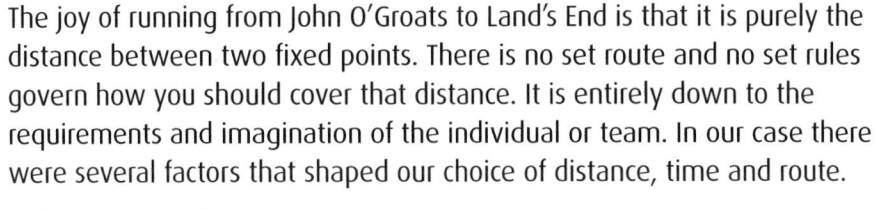

The joy of running from John O'Groats to Land's End is that it is purely the distance between two fixed points. There is no set route and no set rules govern how you should cover that distance. It is entirely down to the requirements and imagination of the individual or team. In our case there were several factors that shaped our choice of distance, time and route.

Many favour LeJog (Land's End to John O'Groats) because the prevailing wind is from behind (SW), but we felt this could be interpreted as an unfair advantage, so we sacrificed this assistance and chose instead to run down the country, thus allowing gravity to do the lion's share. And on the subject of wild beasts, we also had little if no desire to share our run with those timorous beasties of the northern isle - the Scottish midges. As it turned out, we brought the start date forward so this was not an issue. From a totally selfless point of view, ending our run just a single day's drive from home would also mean that should our wives want to witness the end of our heroic, as we like to call it, (foolhardy as they keep referring to it) adventure then it would be much easier for them to do so. Greg of course lives a full day's plane ride from either end of the country, so declared that he was 'not fussed'.

Whichever way you look at it, Land's End to John O'Groats is a very long way. And more than a little hilly (some accounts have stated that it is the equivalent of climbing Everest three times). To be away from family, friends and responsibilities for more than a month was, we felt, too much to ask. We agreed that 30 miles a day could be comfortably sustained with the minimum fear of breakdown. So a direct route of approximately 900 miles or less was required. With the greatest respect and thanks to all those who, with or without their knowledge, offered us their advice, Rory Coleman's 'Jogle Ultra' Race route (with a little tinkering to suit our personal needs) based mainly on 'A' roads, which we felt were probably flatter and more direct, ticked all our boxes. Thank you Rory and thank you for the iPhone tip, you were right of course, it is the answer to nearly all my questions, from navigation to where to camp etc - there really is an APP for everything!

Now chosen, the route was mapped, in a number of different ways. Initially on the computer using MapMyRun (also an App). Once plotted it gave me all sorts of transferable information that was also accessible from the iPhone. Using this information I then marked up the appropriate Landranger maps in daily, thirty mile, sections and started plotting the nearest campsites to our daily stops (which were then booked and, where possible, paid for in advance). I then transferred this information to a Large Scale Road Atlas so that we also had it in a more handy book form. I painstakingly produced two copies, so that Greg had his own and we had a back up if required. One of the many advantages of MapMyRun is that at the press of a button you can print out full, turn by turn, written instructions for the whole route. I broke these down into 30 mile sections and added a map of that section to create daily A4 route pages that would supplement the detailed Landranger map. We could of course also follow the route on Google Maps or MapMyRun using the iPhone. As it turned out we used every version of these route plans throughout the journey.

With the daily distance set we had two issues of sustainability to solve, how to ensure the daily rest we needed and how to restore the daily calories (4500-5500) required? Our tried and tested answer was to break the run into three sections. Three two hour runs with an hour's recovery between each. Enough time to eat and drink, change shoes, socks and kit, check navigation and rest. We also hoped this would keep blisters at bay.

A year before our planned start I set up a blog via OffExploring.com. I chose this site because it also allowed me to make entries via the iPhone. It also linked with Facebook and Twitter so I only needed to upload information once for all to see. The blog was our main means of communication and proved a huge success, generating a great deal of friendly banter which in turn encouraged us greatly. I have included at least one quote from contributions to the blog per day in the narrative.

In addition to the information that was published daily on the blog, the utterly brilliant RAM Tracking supplied a great piece of kit and set up a web page for us (totally free of charge) that enabled friends, family and followers to track our progress minute by minute on a live Google map. Or as my wife said, "You could just watch paint dry!"

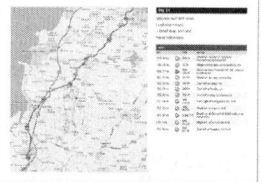

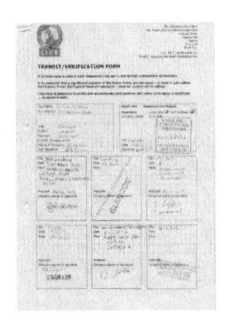

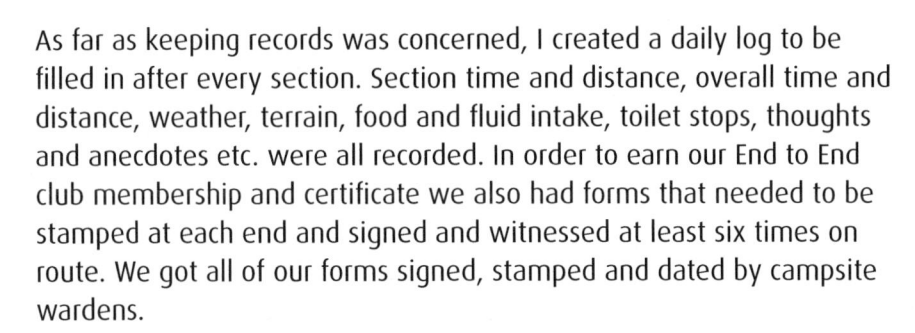

As far as keeping records was concerned, I created a daily log to be filled in after every section. Section time and distance, overall time and distance, weather, terrain, food and fluid intake, toilet stops, thoughts and anecdotes etc. were all recorded. In order to earn our End to End club membership and certificate we also had forms that needed to be stamped at each end and signed and witnessed at least six times on route. We got all of our forms signed, stamped and dated by campsite wardens.

Choosing to use a motorhome afforded us maximum flexibility; transportation, shelter, feeding, sleeping etc. We hired a six berth unit with three permanent beds. Single bunks for JT and myself, and a double bed over the cab for Greg. We elected not to use the toilet or shower. We were pre-booked into campsites every night so that we had full shower block facilities and also access to washing machines. We wore several layers of kit and made three, sometimes four, changes of clothes a day so it was important to be able to wash and dry clothing each night. The campsite also supplied us with electricity and fresh water, when required, and replacement gas cylinders.

Before setting off on the journey I should also perhaps just explain about the 'Wobble on the Jogle Card'. Introduced by JT as a life line to normality, each team member had one card to play each week (they were not allowed to be carried over). The card allowed a request that couldn't be refused (a bath, B&B, steak dinner etc). Only two were played, both involved food and both benefitted us all.

For those inspired to make, or already planning, such a trip, rather than bore the valued reader here or in the narrative, I have included a series of appendices at the back with more detailed information about training, nutrition, route planning, kit, Apps, useful reading and contacts etc. which I hope you may find helpful.

I think the rest is fairly well explained as we go along, so with your permission, and no further delay, let me introduce you to the team.

The main characters

John E Turner (JT). If Carlsberg made best friends... quite simply the most honest, kindly, patient, generous, supportive guy you could ever want to meet. I can't think of a better person to tackle this challenge with and I was so glad when he said yes. And even gladder when his wife, Maz, said yes! What JT doesn't know about long distance running and its history probably isn't worth knowing. Add that knowledge to his physical experience of this crazy sport, along with his generosity of spirit and you have the perfect running partner - this guy is quietly infectious, you have been warned.

100+ marathons
25+ Ultras
Including:
17 x London to Brighton
2 x Comrades (up & down!)
4 x 24hr Track races (best: 116 miles, twice!)

Greg Dwyer. Without Greg none of this would have happened. Greg was my first running partner back in 1997. We met when he was over here teaching for a year. When he returned to Australia he told me I should join a club. JT was the man who welcomed me on my first night. The rest as they say is history. So in short - it's all Greg's fault. Greg was a keen and gifted runner until injury forced him to focus on cycling. Now he is a very keen and extremely gifted (and successful) Mountain Bike racer. As soon as he heard my plan he volunteered to fly halfway across the world, at his own expense, to help. What a friend. His experience of multiday events, wicked humour coupled with his experience of working with kids makes him the perfect man for the job.

3 peaks race competitor (UK & Australia)
Multisport Athlete
12 Ultra Marathons
1 x 24 Hr Mtb Race
2 x 12 Hr Mtb Races
Multi-Day Mtb Racer
1 official Marathon

Peter Rogers. As for me... I am not a gifted runner, I certainly didn't inherit any running genes. The mirror tells me that I am not the required shape, definitely Labrador not Greyhound. I just enjoy running. Most of my friends think I'm mad - and that's OK. My medical notes officially describe me as 'the extreme end of normal'. And I like that.

100+ marathons
12 Ultras
Including:
6 x London to Brighton
2 x Comrades (up & down!)
24hr Track race (104 miles)

My personal motivation

"Why?" Is usually the first question people ask when you tell them what you are doing. But the standard reply, "Because it's there" just isn't enough for me. And it's certainly not sufficient to carry you nearly 900 miles, climbing and descending the equivalent height of Everest, not just once, but three times - allegedly.

I don't have Parkinson's, but the person I hold most dear, my mother, does. Every day, with grace, dignity and great humour she faces this debilitating condition. To begin with things didn't appear so bad. A slight shake was all she had to bear and she found ways to overcome this when necessary. But over the years her opponent began showing his cards. Loss of balance, flexibility, memory, the ability to swallow, occasional difficulty with speech and sudden freezing . Mum's world has gradually got smaller and smaller. There is no set pattern to Parkinson's. Each player holds a different hand and each game is unique. But I don't think it's a game we should be playing at all. The Cure Parkinson's Trust was set up by four people with Parkinson's and they believe that there is a cure to be found. The immediate problem is funding trials, and so that is what money raised from this challenge (including this book) will go directly towards - funding an exciting new trial which could lead to a cure in the future. That's my motivation.

The daily struggle that JT and I will face to put one foot in front of the other is nothing in comparison to the daily effort that many with Parkinson's have to battle with just to maintain their daily lives. For the same period of time that I have been running my mother has fought the condition, with dignity and great humour. It's time to do what I can to make a difference.

'The best way to predict the future is to create it.'

Stephen Covey

The Cure Parkinson's Trust
Charity Number : 1111816

'End to End is the longest challenge you can do in the UK. It's a tough ordeal that takes dedication and commitment.
I greatly admire Peter and John for their courage and desire to achieve this goal. Dig deep, support 'The Cure Parkinson's Trust' and follow their adventure to achieving success.'

Sharon Gayter
Broke the LEJOG World Record in 2006

Start Day -2 | London - Ardlui

Leaving home

The alarm was set for 5.00am, but it wasn't needed! Greg slept in the van, which was parked outside our house overnight. I woke him at ten past with a mug of tea. We packed the last few bits before John and Maz pulled into the street at a quarter to six, just as planned.

The first team challenge was how to stick our magnetic fundraising signs onto the van? A great time to discover that it's made of aluminium! Hmm, have to think about that one.

Scheduled to leave at six to ensure a clear route through London, we pulled away at a quarter past. The plan worked (better than the magnetic signs!) and we made good time getting to the M1, stopping near Luton for breakfast. We all enjoyed a hearty full English breakfast and a bucket of coffee each (thank goodness Greg didn't order large!). Back on the road the satnav finally agreed to show us the way once we recognised Scotland as another country (I'm not going there, the discussion I mean not the country, of course I'm going to the country, and apparently by four o'clock! If you believe in satnavs?)

The weather, slightly chilly, but blue sky and sunshine makes me wish we were running. It would certainly help the nerves. I have to confess to that awful condemned man feeling that one gets before all ultra races. Just have to let them take their course.

Our second stop was for lunch and fuel near Stafford, where we took the opportunity to put some of the signs up with gaffa tape. Once back on the road (with our fundraising mission now clear to all) it was plain sailing all the way to the border at about three o'clock, where we paused once again to refuel. I thought I'd planned for everything, but the biggest challenge to our success is an unforeseen threatened fuel drivers' strike which keeps causing panic buying. We are refuelling as often as possible. In the event of a strike Greg assures me he has a plan, I really hope I never have to discover what it is.

We bought coffees at the garage and Greg made the mistake of putting sweetener in JT's, so to mask his mistake we put a sugar in as well. JT said it was perfect and just how he liked it!

We pressed on, through Glasgow, where I made a wrong turn and had to double back through the suburbs. Thank goodness for the satnav.

'Some of the world's greatest feats were accomplished by people not smart enough to know they were impossible.'

Doug Larson

21 April 2012

The next time we camp here and see this view we will have run 240 miles!

Steve Forsdick
Good luck men. It is a massive challenge and I will be following with interest, I can't wait to hear all your stories.

Mind you, if it hadn't been for the satnav we wouldn't have gone wrong in the first place! Finally free of Glasgow we drove on up the west side of Loch Lomond to our rest for the night, The Ardlui Hotel, Marina & Caravan Park, which we promptly overshot! Travelling a mile or so further along a narrow road with a high stone wall to the left and a long queue of traffic building up behind, I was glad to see a hotel carpark and pulled in to make a U turn. Apparently I narrowly missed a parked motorbike and Range Rover, but I wasn't a witness to this because I was driving and didn't see them! Greg kindly volunteered to drive us back to the Hotel.

We are parked near the water's edge and it's beautiful. My youngest son Maff (19) saw the pictures we took and e-mailed to say he was extremely jealous. He would really love to be here with us on this adventure. Next time Maff! I have absolutely no doubt that he could run it.

Waves of anxiety about this challenge keep hitting me, with palpable force now. I'm sure it's only pre-match nerves. I would like to have told Sue how I was feeling, but I didn't want to worry her. Then, as if she knew, we received a good luck e-mail from Sharon Gayter, encouraging us, amongst other things, 'to let the nerves settle'…truly wonderful timing and so appropriate. Sharon speaks from experience as she broke the Women's End to End record in 2006. We are honoured to have her valued support. Only now is it really beginning to dawn on me just how big this is.

It's been a very long day and none of us got much sleep last night, so after a pre-prepared spaghetti bolognaise (thanks Sue) we are all in bed by 9.45!

Start Day -1 | **Ardlui - John O'Groats**

The end of the beginning

'Champions do not become champions when they win the event, but in the hours, weeks, months and years they spend preparing for it.'

T. Alan Armstrong

Today, the alarm was set for 7.30am, but we were all woken by the sound of heavy rain at ten past six. I believe we all slept well, although Greg did say it had been raining since half two.

At eight fifty-nine (approximately!) we started on the final push (240 miles) to John O'Groats. Greg says I'm not allowed to drive today. I'd like to think it is so I can rest before my epic effort, but in reality I think it's more likely to be something to do with the £1,000 excess if I damage the van. The reader may decide.

Just four miles north of the campsite we glimpsed our first snow. Fortunately, still only on the mountains. It's beautiful and awe inspiring, but also a touch daunting. We stopped in a lay-by at the gateway to the Highlands to take in the panoramic view. While we were there a man in full Scottish dress, complete with bagpipes, emerged from his caravan and stood by the road, placing his cap on the ground! Canny these Scots.

Our first stop was in Fort William for a £1 shop and coffee in the carpark (and a wee in the hedge!) Greg came back with his arms full of useful(?) and necessary(?) items and his face beaming. It doesn't appear to take much to make him happy. I wonder how long it will last?

Yet again we are enjoying glorious sunshine with patches of blue and no wind. I fervently hope we are enjoying similar weather when we return this way in a few days time.

Our lunch break was in the beautiful Fort Augustus, at the foot of Loch Ness. We bought fish and chips from the politest shopkeeper in the world! It was here that we finally caught up with Rory Coleman and most of his 'Jogle Ultra' race runners. It was a very jovial meeting of like minds. Such a shame that our friend Katherine had to pull out soon into day two after a really impressive start. We wished each other luck and left in opposite directions. They had twenty miles left of a fifty mile day followed by thirteen more days to the finish, we have one hundred and fifty more miles to the start then twenty nine days to the finish!

Since Ardlui this morning we have followed the route that we will run. It's useful to see the terrain, but it does little to settle the nerves. If truth be told, it's probably made them worse.

When we finally arrived at John O'Groats, at 6.20pm, everything was

22 April 2012

closed. Office, hotel, campsite. I rang the number pinned to the office door and spoke to the warden's wife. A short while later he turned up, shook me firmly by the hand, sneezed violently, several times, wiped his nose with the same hand, then told me he had a stinker! Oh great!

We had planned to run the short distance from Duncansby Head (just 1.8 further miles up the road) which is the most North Eastern point, so that we could say we'd run the full diagonal, but time really was against us. We needed to eat and organise things, so we ditched the plan in favour of a slightly more relaxed evening.

Mobile phone reception was extremely bad on the edge of the world, and only very faint wi-fi (little did we know at this point that this was really quite good!) so I was unable to publish a proper blog. I promised to make it up to everyone when we were more sorted, had more time and a better signal.

By the time I'd laid out my clothes and kit for the morning, played a game of hunt the tracker unit (yes I know), briefed Greg and handed over the reins, along with map books and the 'bible' - my ring-binder of absolutely everything and anything Jogle orientated, it was nearly half past ten and well past our planned bed time.

I didn't sleep a wink. I have never felt so nervous. I spent the whole night thinking of an acceptable way out. It's a good job I didn't pack my passport!

Colin from Taz

Go for it guys! Have checked out GPS tracker. It is working brilliantly. It shows that you have left it in a bar in Everthorpe Road, South London! Oh well we will have to rely on the blog only for journey verification. Then again if they can fake a moon landing...

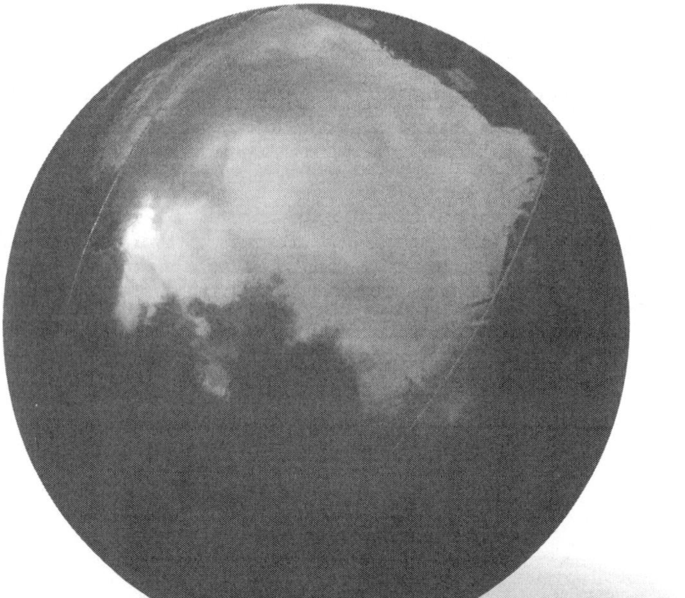

Dear Peter and John,

The hard training is done, the organisation complete, the big day has arrived. Let the nerves settle, eat well, think of the challenge ahead, the money you will raise, the experience of a lifetime, the long hard road, the challenge of the goal, getting up tired every morning, collapsing every night knowing that you are a day nearer achieving your dream. There will be hard times, fun times, painful times, and pleasure times. Go and live your dream, run well, run easy and the joy and satisfaction of finishing will live with you forever.

I hope the weather stays good for you to help you on the way, I will be watching and will try and catch up with you if I can.

Good luck and keep going!

Sharon Gayter

Opposite: The 'real' red ball, our daily finish marker, that we eagerly chased down the country

Day 1 — John O'Groats - Lybster

Finally on the road

Following a night of much rain and very little sleep the alarm eventually sounded at seven o'clock. Finally allowing us to set aside the nocturnal nerves and face the challenge head on.

The wind dropped and the rain stopped just twenty minutes before we stepped out of the van, nerves now replaced by excitement and a keen sense of adventure. A huge, and very welcome, surprise for me on such a grey morning, was the presence of a small group of people to see us off, secretly organised by JT via the internet. Local runner, Alison Smith, brought a couple of fellow runners, Jimmy and Sandy, from her club to the start along with James Mowat, and his wife, from the local Parkinson's group. In addition to all of this, she also organised for Peter Dymond to arrive an hour early to set up the famous End to End Signpost so that we could set off as close to nine as possible.

Anxious not to injure ourselves, we made our way, very carefully, across slippery rocks to the water's edge to dip our fingers in the North Sea, we chose not to get our feet wet! Then we picked up a pebble each to carry with us and throw in the sea at the end of our journey, should we make it that far. Then back to the signpost for our official photo against a heavy grey sky and the long awaited start.

A hearty "5 - 4 - 3 - 2 - 1" countdown from our new friends and a loud blow of the horn from James - and JT and I were on our way, amusingly in different directions for a moment! And yes it's on video!

At last - after three years of planning and seventeen years training on my part, and thirty years for JT, we are on our way. All nerves gone, just the thrill of running now.

We enjoyed a good first day. 80% was uphill, which was good because it helped to slow us down. We had sunshine, rain, a cold breeze and two downpours of hail. So Greg and the van were a welcome sight at both

Chatting to our new friends at a cold and windy, but dry, start

'To-morrow, and to-morrow, and to-morrow, Creeps in this petty pace from day to day.'

William Shakespeare
(Born & Died 23 April)
Macbeth Act 5, scene 5, 19–28

23 April 2012

30 miles

our stops. We've chosen to break our daily run into three sections with an hour break between each one in order to take on food and drink and a change of clothes. Each day's run requires around five thousand calories and it would be impossible to replace these throughout the day in amounts that will still enable us to run. Coffee, peanut butter and jam sandwiches, crisps, chocolate raisins and a change of clothes and we were off again within the planned hour.

In our first session we ran past a sign announcing a forthcoming football match, Wick v Keith. Seemed very unfair on Keith, unless he was a particularly large man, large enough to fill a goalmouth perhaps?

Arriving at the thirty mile finish point, we were greeted by two lovely ladies, Wendy and her mum, who had been following us on the blog and wanted to come out to support us and give us a donation. The perfect way to end our first day.

A short drive to the campsite (with the BEST showers in the world). An opportunity to wash kit, refuel properly and catch up with the administration, including writing the all important blog and the first day was a complete success.

Well perhaps not a complete success. I managed to lose the charger for my Garmin, but luckily brought a spare. And according to the tracker (which we did find last night) we haven't actually left home yet, leading to theories that our whole trip might just be a hoax to rival the Moon Landings. James Taylor (no not THE James Taylor, although he is of course THE James Taylor to us) from RAM Tracking, who organised it, will be working on getting the site up and running very soon so that family, friends and supporters can see exactly where we are at any time of night or day. I do hope we are not going to regret this! Please let me assure all readers that we are indeed just where we say we are! See pic above right of us with 'our' red ball finish marker, which is working!

Need some sleep tonight as we face another hilly 30 miles tomorrow.

So - the facts: 30 miles down, 830 to go! Popular opinion holds that it's down hill from here, but in reality Land's End is higher, by 57m.

Session 1
11.6m 1:57.18

Session 2
23.09m 3:53.11

Session 3
30.05m 5:08.35

Marathon: 4:30.05

Bernie
Well done guys, look forward to your updates and hope all goes well. I've put the kettle on so don't be long will you?

Day 2 — **Lybster - Brora**

All hail the weather!

Delighted to realise that we are beginning to find a daily morning ritual already. JT at one end, me at the other, and Greg staying in his nest above the cab until it's safe to climb down.

Sadly, we were unable to find the Garmin charger last night, but thankfully I brought a spare GPS. Great forward planning! So after a brief read of the instructions and a couple of trial runs (literally) we were off.

It was certainly no dry run! Yet another day of rain and more hail. We could see it coming in from the sea like a huge grey curtain. It's extremely difficult to know what to wear. One minute we are generating heat, the next we are cold and wet. I guess we are going to have to get used to this. I still think it's the hardest part of long distance running, deciding on the appropriate clothing for the day.

Greg left the van and cycled back to us with more drink and the key so we could let ourselves in while he went for a long ride.

Arriving at the van we discovered he'd tucked it up exceedingly close to a brick wall. We could only assume he'd exited via the passenger's door, to which we didn't have a key. We were forced to squeeze in through the side door, a manoeuvre that would present us with little problem in a couple of weeks time when we have lost some weight!

Greg arrived back before we left, having enjoyed a cup of tea with a group of four cyclists who had passed us earlier, on their final leg to John O'Groats. We'd been a bit upset when the lead cyclist informed us that we only had 860 miles (our total projected distance) to go! So much for the first day's run!

Our second leg was better than expected. I was cold at the beginning and keen to keep warm. We decided at

Cold and wet, but very visible in our Hi-viz Hexx sponsored running vests

---

'Some people want it to happen, some wish it would happen, others make it happen.'

Michael Jordan

I kid you not...

Brora was the first place in the north of Scotland to have electricity, giving rise to the local nickname of "Electric City".

What we need is "Wi-Fi City"!

24 April 2012

60 miles

the start we would walk steep hills, to conserve energy (it would also probably be quicker). By the end of these two days we have walked six steep hills and at the foot of each one it has begun to rain and at the top it has stopped! How does this work? It's a real problem, because it means we get cold and wet and our body temperature drops.

Greg was parked at our first border crossing - Caithness into Sutherland. He took our photo and we 'jogled' on down a wonderful sweeping hill that breathed fresh life into our legs. When we met Greg at the border we asked him to drive over distance to our second rest stop so that we had over twenty-three miles done, leaving just under seven for the last run of the day.

Seeing the campsite was just a short distance further on from our planned finish, we decided to run the whole way. We were both very tired, but happy. We achieved some good running today, given the weather and hills. We knew before we started this would be a hard one. I'm still finding it difficult to eat enough food, but I drank a lot more today, and feel I got that balance right, so I'll focus on food tomorrow. Eating each break (sandwiches, crisps, fruit etc) is not a problem, it's just the large meal in the evening that's hard to get down. I may need to try and eat sooner after the run, or perhaps try two smaller meals.

We continued to have problems with wi-fi and phone signals, so Greg suggested a drive to the local pub to write the blog and catch up with messages. It was only after we crossed the carpark that both JT and I realised that we were still both wearing our slippers! Greg took a photo of course. Inside the pub (where no one took the slightest interest in our footwear) we found the four cyclists that we had met earlier, enjoying a celebratory meal with their support crew (who we hadn't met). During the evening we discovered that two of the cyclists had done the trip before, by para-glider, in four days! Maybe we're not so weird?

> **So - the facts:** A good day's running, despite the hills and weather, we ran long, eventually finishing in 5:47, having run 31.78 miles. 60 miles in total. We are now in Sutherland.

Session 1
11.4m 2:02.13

Session 2
23.52m 4:19.02

Session 3
31.78m 5:47.23

Marathon: 4:47.08

Steve Forsdick
Keep it up gents. Glad you found the pub, you can find all sorts of inspiration there. Will get on your fund raising page!

25

Day 3 | **Brora - Golspie**

Long and windy road

'Sometimes success is due less to ability than to zeal.'

Charles Buxton

We were kept awake half the night with heavy rain, which was still going strong when the alarm went off (Sonny & Cher's 'I got you babe'!) It prompted us to discuss different approaches to the day, such as running single hours, but in the end Greg just said he would stay nearby. As it turned out, we ran the entire day without a single drop of rain, shame we couldn't say the same about the wind.

Our mettle was seriously tested in our second session, on a kilometre-long bridge across the Dornoch Firth. We were grateful it had high side rails or I don't think we would have attempted it. We tightened the clasps on our caps and just went for it. Our reward for making it to the halfway point was our third county - Ross & Cromarty. No time to celebrate or we risked being blown back into Sutherland! As it turned out, that was the easy bit (wish we'd known!). Turning left off the bridge we were faced with not just a strong head wind but a steep, sweeping, mile long hill to the van. Unable to even hear one another speak, we just went heads down for it again.

Our first session of the day was no less of a struggle. The A9 narrowed, forcing us to jump up, along and then down off the high grass verge in order to avoid the fast on coming cars and lorries. Not only did it break our rhythm, it required more energy and a great deal more concentration, leaving us quite tired after our first two hour section.

Michael enjoying the warmth of the van, and a well earned cup of tea

We met our first End to End walker today, Michael Waters. When our paths crossed, in our first break, he had been walking nine hours a day for forty-eight days. An absolutely superb effort. Greg offered him tea and a chat in the van, which he seemed delighted to accept. So we are not the only nutcases out here!

Because we ran almost two miles over distance yesterday (in order to reach the campsite) we only needed to run a little over 28 miles today. So by the time we finished our second section, up a steep hill, into a very strong wind, our reward was a shorter, just over 5 mile, run before our day was over.

25 April 2012

90 miles

Hopping into the van, Greg shuttled us back to Tain for the night. The showers were so cold, and the wind so strong, that after trekking to the block I decided, in the interest of health (and probably safety) not to take my clothes off in this environment. I retreated back to the motorhome to help Greg with the washing up and then a brief chat on the phone to my youngest son Maff. He was planning to come and find us near Lockerbie, but sadly he's decided to visit Paris instead. I told him we didn't go near Paris, but he said it was cheaper! Family eh!

Tracking update: the wonderful James Taylor at RAM Tracking, who has been working hard to solve the problem, has identified a faulty chip at our end, so he is sending a new tracker overnight to our next campsite, so we should be back on the map by Friday morning.

> **So - the facts:** Today, the number of miles we are chasing dropped from a number beginning with an eight to a number beginning with a seven. We crossed our third border, Ross & Cromarty, and we have now run 90 miles. Tonight we are camped by the Falls of Shin and tomorrow we start from the Sands of Nigg. You really couldn't make this stuff up!

"We're only bloody doing it!"

Session 1
11.74m 1:56.56

Session 2
22.68m 3:51.49

Session 3
27.45m 4:40.07

Marathon: 4:28.18

Caroline

Hi guys. Thinking of you at lunch time when the 'Road Scarf' passed the 100th row, which means you've passed your 100th mile. Sending you both warm hugs to offset those Scottish gales.

Caroline is knitting a scarf representing our journey, 30 rows a day for 29 days. Just Brilliant!

Day 4 **Golspie - Beauly**

Verging on the ridiculous

It was a good day today. The forecast was not good - but what rain we experienced was carried by a strong North Easterly - so it swept us along and didn't blow the cold wet stuff in our faces.

What did get in our faces was the traffic on the infernal A9. What a nightmare this road is. It was even narrower today, which meant even less space to avoid the cars and lorries hurtling towards us. In the end it wasn't the ones we could see that were the problem, but the ones we couldn't. JT and I had been running single file inside the white line, facing the traffic, but three cars in five minutes chose to overtake from behind, at speed, and came very very close to taking us out. JT saw them and I felt them. John was amazed I still had a left arm, er left. So for the rest of our journey up the A9 we had to hop up and down off the verge, which was murder on the legs.

In all this madness, Greg somehow managed to find a small lay-by on the A9 in which to squeeze the motorhome. Goodness knows how he got into it at speed. Every time lorries went by the whole van rocked quite violently. We elected to get out via the passenger's door!

Soon after we set off, JT realised he'd forgotten his water bottle, so we sheltered under a bridge a couple of miles further up the road to ring back to the van and ask Greg to catch us up. We met just the other side of the Cromarty Firth, a road bridge about three quarters of a mile in length. Leaving the van with replenished supplies we had just two and a half steep uphill miles of the A9 remaining before we finally, and with great celebration, bade farewell. We took a photo and shook hands! After four days the A9 is finally behind us. A kind word to those considering Land's End to John O'Groats, is this really how you want to spend the last few days of your journey? Just a thought.

The 'B' road that we now followed (a revised route that got us off the A9

No hard shoulder, high and very rough grass verges, huge lorries travelling at equally huge speeds throwing up huge amounts of spray - boy we're going to miss this road

'Success is to be measured not so much by the position that one has reached in life as by the obstacles which one has overcome while trying to succeed.'

Booker T. Washington

26 April 2012

120 miles

early) was a total breath of fresh air. We soon met up with Greg for 'proper' break two and then we only had about seven miles, through exceptionally pleasant farmland and woods to Beauly and then onto the campsite, through a majestic avenue of trees and over an old stone bridge.

Before arriving we had been concerned because there was supposed to be no washing facilities, but on arrival, much to our delight, we were informed that there were - but in the ladies! Not sure what this means, readers draw your own conclusions because I'm not going there. It must be something about Scotland!

A lovely meal (thanks Greg) then we headed off to the campsite bar, where we spent a very pleasant evening in front of a roaring fire, with a lovely Welsh barman called Graham, sounds like the first line of a Limerick?!

Graham tells us that snow is forecast for tomorrow - hmmm, we'll have to see.

So - the facts: A mile before our first break we reached the 100 mile mark and at mile 109 - WE LEFT THE A9! after four days.

Session 1
12.18m 2:00.35

Session 2
23.08m 3:56.34

Session 3
29.79m 5:04.42

Marathon: 4:28.30

Steve Freemantle

Hi guys. Glad to hear you had a good day, my admiration is total. Tell the Aussie whimp to cycle whatever the weather!!

A couple of pints with the canniest Welsh barman in Scotland, then home to bed

29

Day 5 — **Beauly - Fort Augustus**

Loch Ness... a Monster

Awoke this morning to blue sky and white clouds, for the first time... giving us hope that the forecast for snow later in the day might be wrong.

Our first eleven mile section took us through some stunning scenery on an undulating road which we found quite hard going. JT spotted a sign hanging by a garden gate, in the middle of absolutely nowhere, that gave us the most extraordinarily precise distance to Land's End, 732 miles! We had to stop and take a photo.

We both experienced difficulty getting the wheels turning during the first session, so we were glad to see Greg at the top of a steep hill. A short chat gave us the encouragement we needed to see it through. He's a great motivator. We knew we would be walking up some hills, but we never expected to be walking down. In the last couple of miles there were two 15% hills that were so steep they jarred our calves and quads to such an extent that we were forced to walk sideways!

Section two was the one we had been looking forward to, all along the north shore of Loch Ness. It had rained during the break, but the sun came out as we headed off and gave us a stunning introduction to the Loch, beginning with a wonderful view of Urquhart Castle. We then enjoyed a couple more miles of rolling road until the heavens

'If you start to feel good during an ultra, don't worry you will get over it.'

Gene Thibeault

I kid you not...

Along with a monster Loch Ness also contains more fresh water than all the lakes in England and Wales combined.

And we know where all that water comes from... the sky!

Urquhart Castle in the sunshine on Loch Ness, just before it started snowing!

27 April 2012

150 miles

It will be interesting to see if it's true!

opened and heavy sleet, then the forecast snow fell. From then on it was cold, wet, undulating hills with blind bends, but beautiful waterfalls, forest and mountains. Greg had decided to ride the Loch during this session and gave us the key to let ourselves in. He returned early though, because of the weather and lorries - a real shame. I really want Greg to get as much cycling out of this trip as possible. The break didn't seem long enough and we headed off to Fort Augustus, all too ready to end the day. The road took us inland to cross a river, which was a shame, but we were soon back with the Loch and in sight of home. Despite the conditions we ran long again in order to reach the camp site and were delighted to be met by Greg and the red ball featuring a huge '150' for the final photo of the day.

We stopped in Fort Augustus on our way to the start and bought fish and chips, so while we showered, Greg cycled off to the same shop and bought chips for all. A practical and appropriate way to end the day's run.

I loved Loch Ness, and I'd really been looking forward to today since I mapped the route, it was just such a shame that the weather was so bad and the traffic so fast with steep rises and blind bends. Not really a sightseeing tour, just a hard day which took a lot out of us, leaving us very cold and wet.

So - the facts: 150 miles covered and we are now over a sixth of the way there. This evening we ran long so in the morning we start with a mile and a half in hand. Tomorrow we head for Fort William (the last time I was there was to climb a mountain - absolutely no danger of that this time!)

Session 1
11.47m 2:07.26

Session 2
22.98m 4:19.34

Session 3
31.00m 5:50.53

Marathon: 4:54.22

Cliff Keen

Just caught up with your first 5 days. You seem to be in great shape, physically & mentally - a testament to your training. Keep the blogs coming and the legs turning.

Day 6 | **Fort Augustus - Fort William**

Time and time again

Morning routines are becoming more relaxed, as we get into the rhythm of what we are doing.

Greg drove us to our start at the entrance to the campsite, then left us to drive twelve miles further on. To save time I had captured the satellites before we set off, as Greg always makes sure we are OK before leaving us. We waved goodbye, pressed the button and the watch said 'NO!' It actually said 'Memory Full', but same thing! I tried a couple of times, but to no avail. So JT and I sat on a bench to try and work out the appropriate sequence of buttons to press and I called Greg to stop him going any further in case I needed the instruction booklet. The phone just went to voice-mail. Five more minutes of experimentation and I finally managed to wipe the memory and the watch was kind enough to let us proceed. I left JT on the bench and retraced our steps, pressed the button and picked him up as I ran past. So we were fifteen minutes late starting, but so what? It's a challenge not a race!

Finally on our way, we 'jogled' up the long climb out of Fort Augustus, which made sure we didn't shoot off too quickly. Not that there was too much danger of that after yesterday's run. Even if it had been downhill! Frost was still lying in the shade, but it was warm in the sunshine and we paused to take photos of the snow topped mountains.

Crossing the Caledonian Canal we walked a hill, then descended past clear, still water, that perfectly reflected the trees and mountains on the other side. Just stunning! We encouraged a group of End to End cyclists who were heading for John O'Groats, now just a day's ride away. A few moments later, one of them returned to ride along side us and offer us encouragement for a while before turning to catch up

'There is a powerful driving force inside every human being that once unleashed, can make any vision, dream or desire a reality.'

Tony Robbins

The beautiful Loch Lochy

28 April 2012

180 miles

with his friends. There is an extraordinary bond between End to Enders. His interest and kindness certainly put the spring back in our step.

Not long after this we met Greg, who had cycled back to meet us. He gave us the key then chased off after the cyclists. He rode with them a while before joining them for a coffee. We were so pleased the weather had changed, allowing Greg to enjoy some great cycling and views at last.

Break one over, we set off again. Stopping almost immediately to take more pictures of Loch Lochy. Breathtaking. We followed it's shore line for almost an hour before finally heading in and up towards the Commando Memorial which stands at the top of a winding pass with the most wonderful panorama of snow-capped mountains. We stopped here briefly on our way up in order to take a few photos, but today's view was even more glorious, with blue sky and fresh snow dusting the peaks.

We ran swiftly down the pass, and up and down the hills that finally led us into Fort William. Once again we elected to run long, to a point nearer the campsite, but it turned out to be two miles further than we thought, and it rained for both of them! So not one of our better choices.

1 Wobble on the Jogle

But Greg made a good choice, he played his 'Wobble on the Jogle' card and requested a steak dinner in a restaurant. But bad choice of recommended steak restaurant as steak was off! But good choice of hotel just over the road, where steak was on, along with badly needed wi-fi. Although bad choice if you wanted a warm friendly welcome! I don't think it was because JT and I were still in our slippers!

So - the facts: 180 miles down, nearly halfway through Scotland, and into our fourth county - Invernesshire.

Session 1
11.68m 2:07.32

Session 2
21.60m 3:58.01

Session 3
30.07m 5:23.57

Marathon: 4:44.05

Apples
Pete and John, Enjoy the beauty of the Highlands (anything to take your minds off the legs)! Hope the weather is holding for you - day of rain here! Fantastic effort - keep it up.

33

Day 7　　**Fort William - Altnafeadh**

All things come to pass

'Stadiums are for spectators. We runners have nature and that is much better.'

Juha Vaatainen

Apparently, seven days running, makes one week! But not us, if anything it's making us fitter!

I really didn't think today could beat yesterday, but it did, by 30 miles! We awoke to a clear blue sky with not a cloud in sight, and none appeared all day. We were apprehensive about today because we were due to run the Glen Coe Pass, a climb that purported to be 14% in places.

The first run was quite quiet, running through Fort William, along the waterfront, where the water was so still it was like a mirror. We were in stride, but both holding back because we knew what the final two legs had in store.

We met Greg outside a tea shop. JT saw a young couple at a bus stop and jumped out to rattle the Parkinson's tin. They were delighted to talk and gave us some money. Two minutes before we were due to leave, a car screeched to a halt in front of us. An ex-military man jumped out and ran to the door. He'd seen the van and wanted to donate. We had a quick chat and gave him some of our sponsorship cards which he promised to share with his running clubmates.

On the road again. Approaching a girder bridge I felt a sharp twinge across the top of my left foot. We stopped to take a photo of the Pass from the bridge and continued, but it was a spasm pain and I had to walk for a while. It continued all day, despite icing at the next stop. I'm really hoping it's just a niggle and that ice and a night's rest will sort it out.

The sun continued to shine and the road began to climb. We decided to run what we could. In the end the scenery was too inspiring and we reckon we must have run a good 90% of the Pass.

Greg had parked the van in the same carpark we stopped in to take pictures on the way up to John O'Groats. He'd given us the key earlier on, because he was cycling up and down and around the pass most of the day. As it turned out he was in the van with lunch and snacks all prepared. What a hero! Words really can't praise this guy enough.

He left us to lock up and headed off up the Pass again to check out the final stopping point, six and a half miles further on. We met him on the way up to the plateau at the top and he warned us that we might want to stop and take a picture. Boy was he right. The most amazing view of

29 April 2012

210 miles

the valley and road ahead, stretching out for miles and miles. This really was a run we didn't want to end, but we knew we must be wise.

We enjoyed four or so miles of sweeping downhill, across a small bridge and then as the road began to rise we saw the van parked by a white pyramid sign.

Enough was enough, it really had been the best day, we could only hope for the same sun tomorrow, to finish the job off.

> **So - the facts:** 210 miles done, we are just over halfway through Scotland and a quarter of the way to our final destination. Our highest weekly mileage, ever!
>
> Tomorrow we camp at the same campsite in Ardlui that we stayed in on the way up. It hardly seems possible.

Session 1
12.20m 2:09.08

Session 2
23.34m 4:32.08

Session 3
29.43m 5:44.06

Marathon: 5:08.48

Jim and Ron
Hi guys you will no doubt be jogging very hard, hope all going well and you still have good weather. Thanks for the help in fixing our bike hope everything goes well regards - Jim.

35

Day 8 Altnafeadh - Inverarnan

It's tough at the top

It's not very often you can trust the weather forecast to be absolutely 100% accurate. It's difficult to say which surprised me the most, the weather or the timing?

It rained all evening, all night and it was still raining when we left the campsite to drive back up the Pass to our starting point for the day. The forecast promised it would stop raining before we started our run at 9.00am. As we climbed out of the van at 9.00am on the dot, it stopped raining - and started to snow! We left the Garmin outside to lock onto satellites and retreated back into the van to put on more clothes, woolly hats and most important of all, lights, as the cloud was also very low. The mountains we saw so clearly yesterday were now invisible as we reluctantly stepped out into a blizzard. We agreed a meeting point eleven miles up the road, but asked Greg to stay close, in case we needed to call him back due to the cold, -1.2c. What a difference a day makes!

It would have been all too easy to let the elements get to us, extreme conditions call for extreme measures - so to keep our spirits up we sang songs into the wind at the top of our voices. It worked for me. I'm not sure JT fully appreciated my singing or choice of songs, you'll have to read his account to discover that. He certainly seemed to be laughing a lot. The cabaret was brought to an abrupt end when we saw a motorbike that had taken the bend too fast and ended up some distance from the road. Thinking that it might have just happened we stopped to search the surrounding area in case the rider had been thrown clear and was lying injured and unseen. Finding no one, we assumed it had already been dealt with and resumed the running, but not the singing.

Concerned about the weather, Greg had parked halfway through the section to ensure we were OK. We

Assuring Greg that we are OK

'There's no such thing as bad weather, just soft people.'

Bill Bowerman

I kid you not...

Equality at last in the fast food industry:

Burger Queen

36

30 April 2012

240 miles

paused just long enough to demonstrate that we were, take a quick photo and have a brief chat with a solo End to End cyclist heading for John O'Groats. Then it was back to the job in hand.

Now that we were on the open plateau above the Pass there was nothing to shield us from the weather so we were grateful to see Greg once again and finally find shelter from the wind. An hour later we headed off once more, for the hardest session of the day. Mercifully dry now, but with a strong headwind, we faced a six mile incline that took us up and over the next range of hills, and another county border. As we started on the five mile descent we met Greg powering his way up on his bike. Despite his encouragement it was a quiet run down, the morning's run cost a lot of energy and it felt like we were draining the tank. Our spirits were dramatically lifted by two cyclists who shouted "SHAKE, JOGLE & ROLL!" at the top of their voices as they raced past us! Surprised, we were still chuckling when we discovered the van parked just around the corner. Mystery solved! Thanks guys.

Still tired, but eager to polish off the last seven and a half miles, we agreed to walk the hills as we climbed stiffly out of the van. The good news, it turned out to be down hill all the way to the finish. The bad news, it required more energy as the road was so steep it jarred every muscle and bone in the body! Quads screaming and calves throbbing we 'ooohed' and 'ahhhed' our way, quite loudly, all the way to the finish.

A tough day and like the animals and birds in the old 18th century inn we visited in the evening to unwind and find wi-fi! - we were stuffed! Turned out they were the lucky ones, it was also folk night! The pain of the road we can take - but not folk night, so we retreated to the modern comfort of the campsite bar. Which was warm and welcoming (once Greg had used his Australian charm to negotiate our way back in through the locked gates!)

So - the facts: 240 miles in 8 days, we are back in Ardlui, and the border is getting closer. We have also run through our fifth county, Argyll & Bute and into our sixth - Stirling.

Session 1
11.78m 2:05.32

Session 2
22.58m 4:05.15

Session 3
30.07m 5:23.26

Marathon: 4:44.15

Chris Pike
Pick up a couple of paddles if you can chaps... you may need them once you cross the border into droughtland England...it's hissing down! Keep warm and cheerful...

Day 9

Inverarnan - Dumbarton

A pain in the Firkin Point

'Our greatest glory is not in never falling, but in rising every time we fall.'

Confucius

I kid you not...

Halfway through our second run of the day we finally discovered...

The Firkin Point!

Would a change in the weather herald an easier day? Blue sky and sunshine meant we could dispense with our jackets for the first time. And fears that the banks of Loch Lomond might be a repeat of Loch Ness were completely dispelled as they turned out to be every bit as bonny as the song described. It was the banks of the A82 that turned out to be the low road.

The first eleven miles rolled gently along the Loch and we took our time, enjoying the spring sunshine. It was only during our second section (twelve miles) that the (A82) road began to climb. After five miles of constant gradient I began to experience the pain across the top of my left foot and a couple of inches up the shin that I first experienced in the Glen Coe Pass. A further four miles up the hill and it was becoming difficult to run. So during the break, while JT raised £5 by hiring out our spanner to a passing cyclist, I raised and iced my foot.

Sun still shining, we set off once again, but although the sun shone on us, the road didn't. It turned from a broad road with plenty of space to run, into a dual carriageway resembling more of a racetrack. With commuters more focused on getting home quickly than on us we were forced to abandon the road and use the verge. The grass was so long and the ground so uneven that it was impossible to run and almost impossible to walk. We only had six miles to go, but under these conditions it was going to take forever and my foot was really quite painful now, so I rang Greg. As it turned out, Greg could only find a safe place to stop two miles short. It appeared that the A82 was in control and had made the decision for us. We finished short, but only a little short of a mile overall because we ran long yesterday, so not a real problem, unlike my foot.

Once at the campsite, I donned warm gear and waded out into Loch Lomond with a cup of soup, while I waited for our club physio, Nick, to phone with advice. In the meantime, Greg demonstrated his sincere sympathy by taking pictures, and JT smiled and waved from the van. Thanks guys!

Turns out it's an impingement injury, initially brought on by jumping down heavily off the verges on the A9, then aggravated by the long hills we've been running for the past three days. The tendon running

1 May 2012

270 miles

up the front of the foot to the base of the shin is now inflamed and swollen because it's rubbing against the bone. It's an injury that needs to be taken seriously.

Nick gave me two courses of treatment, both impossible. The first was stop running for a few days and let it rest, yeh Ok, like that's an option! The second was anti-inflammatories, but as I have Chronic Kidney Disease this was equally impossible advice to follow. If I choose to carry on, the advice is to lessen the impact by walking all hills and shortening the sections to allow more rest, then elevate and ice at every break.

No prizes for guessing my choice. I'm resting, elevating and icing in the hope that it won't be as bad as the diagnosis makes out. I can't hear any fat ladies singing so I'm guessing it's still game on!

Things look a bit dark at the moment, but tomorrow is another day and I've heard Glasgow in the spring is beautiful.

> **So - the facts:** 270 miles run. We passed into another county, West Dunbartonshire. And most importantly of all, during our second run of the day, for those that might still be wondering, we discovered the Firkin Point!

Session 1
11.21m 2:08.01

Session 2
23.87m 4:35.20

Session 3
28.14m 5:49.58

Marathon: 5:10.03

Eva
John, I love your way to raise money! Made me laugh. Can I hire your hat for £5?

The longer I stood there - the smaller I got...

39

Day 10 | **Dumbarton - Chapelton**

"Dormouse"

Not keen to face six more miles on the A82, we worked out an alternative route that was a tad longer, but easier to run. Easier to run if your foot works - mine didn't. So today we are forced to walk.

When running ultras together, JT and I have a code word - 'Dormouse'. It means, 'I'm going through a bad patch and need to slow down or stop awhile, I am releasing you to go on, it's your choice, I won't be offended if you leave me'. JT was an absolute brick and said he was happy to walk. Can't say I was particularly good company, not knowing if this is an injury that will right itself or is going to be a problem and my time is up. And how does it affect everyone else? I can't see myself throwing in the towel, only if it stops JT from fulfilling his dream. It's a hard one and it tapped the emotions. Reduced to three or three and a half miles an hour, it looked as though it was going to be a very long day. JT and Greg remained upbeat, but it was hard for me to see any light at the end of the tunnel, only I knew how much pain I was in.

Greg provided a not so welcome diversion when we met up on the outskirts of Glasgow. He'd locked the keys in the motorhome, still in the ignition. My AA card was, of course, also in the van. While I phoned Sue to get the number, Greg took the aerial off and managed to push the window latches up. I gave him a bunk-up and launched him through the window so he could reach the door catch. Needless to say, despite being in broad daylight and by a very busy road, no one took the slightest bit of notice. I guess that's Glasgow for you.

Our next diversion was 'hunt the entrance to the Clyde Foot Tunnel'. Having found a locked entrance we walked round in circles asking directions until we ended up back where we started. On closer inspection we discovered a button to press. There was a long pause then the door automatically opened. Immediately closing once we were through, we were trapped in a cage until the next gate opened. If that wasn't scary enough the tunnel itself was the most awful smelling, damp, graffitied subterranean passage you could ever be so unlucky to find, let alone be in. Suffice to say we were most relieved to finally see daylight and press the button for release into the sunshine. What an

'You have a choice. You can throw in the towel, or you can use it to wipe the sweat off your face.'

Anonymous

I kid you not...

Apparently, the security gates have failed a number of times since being fitted in 2009. A fact Greg neglected to pass on...

2 May 2012

300 miles

experience. Certainly not a tunnel I would like to run a marathon in. (Now who would be stupid enough to have actually done that?)

Walking was slow, painful and very frustrating. JT refused to go on ahead so we plodded on at 3mph, more time to enjoy the sunshine! But time was running out, so fresh back from a cultural visit to the Burrell Art Collection, Greg identified and programmed in a much shorter (but more complicated) route on the iPhone that would get us out of Glasgow a lot quicker than the main road. Anything to get us to the finish before dark.

It was obvious we weren't going to finish before eight o'clock, or even later, so Greg parked up in a KFC carpark to cook us dinner, and yes he did have to buy a meal - so we had a starter!

As luck would have it, tonight's campsite was the furthest from our finishing point, just under an hour's drive away. Following such a difficult day, Greg was concerned that we needed as much rest as possible so, while we were completing the last five miles, wearing lights again as the sun was now setting, he searched for a safe place to wild camp. A practice still legal in Scotland.

JT and I were in no fit state to make decisions and were very glad to have Greg make them for us and even happier that the day was over and we could get to bed. It was a close call today, and not one we can face repeating tomorrow. Physio Nick has advised running the flats and downs, if at all possible, to give the foot more recovery time at the end of the day. So we need to consider a new strategy, but that's a decision for tomorrow.

So - the facts: We walked 30.56 miles today to reach the 300 mile target, in almost 13 hours (with breaks). We are now over a third of the way and two and a half days from the border.

Even the Romans gave up at the A82! A large sign at Old Kilpatrick (by the side of the A82) announced that this was the furthest point North West that the Romans reached, the Antonine Wall.

Three more counties today, East Renfrewshire, South Lanarkshire and East Kilbride.

JT is the best mate you could ever wish to have.

Session 1
10.14m 3:18.56

Session 2
18.34m 6:16.00

Session 3
25.61m 8:23.52

Session 4
30.56m 9:49.39

Marathon: 8:32.08

Ben and Lauren

Oh Pete, this made me cry. It's so moving, I really think you should write a book and include these blogs! I really hope your foot gets better, you guys are so inspirational to keep going. Just remember you are a third of the way through!

Day 11   **Chapelton - Crawford**

Time to re-focus

'Suffer now and live the rest of your life a champion.'

Muhammad Ali

Wild camping just 500 metres from the finish/start was a good call. It meant we got a good night's rest and didn't have an hours drive from the campsite, which would have been unneeded pressure after yesterday's exhausting late finish.

It's incredible how the body can revive itself. The revised strategy for today was to cover four mile sections so that if I was still unable to run JT had the option to run on and then have a rest or continue, and I would do what I could - picking up food and drink to eat on the walk. As it happened - after a short walk to warm up the foot I found I could run lightly on it. So running with my right foot toe first (to avoid pressure on my heel which was still complaining about yesterday's long limpy walk) and my left as flat and as light as possible to avoid pain and pressure I was able to shimmy along at an average of ten and a half minute miling.

3 May 2012

330 miles

Thankfully, in this way, we were able to stay together through beautiful, sunny, gently undulating, lowland scenery and run three ten mile sections in an average 2hr 20min, allowing ourselves 45 min breaks to ensure we finished the day relatively early. Which we did with a run/walk time of 7 hrs 3 mins. Not bad for someone who could hardly walk at all yesterday.

Greg really needed a break from the pressure of yesterday, so he went for a long three hour ride while we finished off section two, enjoyed a 45 min break and set out on our final leg of the day. He caught up with us at the twenty five mile mark to replenish our water bottles. The last couple of miles were hard because we were both tired from yesterday and JT's knees suffered on the sharp downs. I really can't tell you how much respect I have for this guy.

The campsite was mercifully near so I was iced and elevated, showered and fed, and iced and elevated again, in what seemed like no time. It's a lovely campsite but, sadly, I have little energy left to explore, although I did manage to hobble to the shower and toilet block which were heaven after last night's free camping.

Our hope is that today's effort will not have caused too much stress and that we will be able to repeat the process tomorrow. It may be slow, but it's great to be running again.

Last night's blog inspired more comments than usual and we were enormously encouraged by messages from friends and family. We really are very grateful for all the support we receive.

> **So - to the facts:** 30.09 miles in 7:03.18 as opposed to yesterday's 9:49.39! Still somewhat slower than our first 30 mile run: 5:08.35, but at least we are back to running and it's so wonderful to be out of Glasgow! Just a day and a half to the border. And on the subject of borders - we are now in Strathaven.

Session 1
10.15m 2:18.01

Session 2
19.89m 4:37.34

Session 3
30.09m 7:03.18

Marathon: 6:04.50

Stan
Allow time at the border - taking 3 hours to enter England at the moment.

Chris
Heel and toe? Don't forget to *'dosey doe'*!

Day 12   **Crawford - Lockerbie**

We'll take the high road

'Running hurts up to a point and then it doesn't get any worse.'

Ann Trason

I kid you not

Man in car:
"Are you end to enders?"

JT and me:
"No - not yet!"

No one wanted to be first out of bed this morning. John and I had to look after ourselves as Greg slept in. He'd been up at four o'clock Skypeing his class back home in Tasmania. He spoke to them about the trip for about half an hour. With ten minutes to go we reluctantly woke him.

Still not certain how the foot will perform, we arranged for Greg to stop at five mile intervals, but when we reached him, we were keen, and able, to carry on for the full ten. The road was very kind to us and we reached ten miles in less than two hours. A 45 minute break and we were on our way again. JT had a difficult second section. My right heel was much better today so I was able to run normally with my right foot, but still had to tap along with the left.

The weather and scenery were terrific, so Greg left the van for us at the twenty mile mark, at the top of a long steep hill, and went for a long sight-seeing tour on his bike, visiting all sorts of places, including the birthplace of Robert the Bruce. He also had time to buy presents for both of us - chocolate fingers for me, and six bottles of local beer for John!

We fed and watered ourselves and got back on this amazing road that we have followed for nearly fifty miles, running parallel to the motorway, but with next to no traffic. It is so lovely not to have to play with the cars and lorries. The service road (as the locals referred to it) led us all the way to Lockerbie, a really beautiful town. The road rolled a bit, but we were quite grateful. By 27 miles my foot is beginning to argue back so needs a little TLC to get it home. We had our closing picture taken under a 300 yards sign that Greg altered to say 360!

Greg initially drove us to the wrong campsite, but when we eventually

Team Greg reflecting by the Loch at our campsite

44

4 May 2012

360 miles

arrived at the right one, what a welcome we got. If ever you are in Lockerbie and need a place to stay you must visit Kirk Loch Caravan & Camping site and ask for Doug. The nicest most generous person in the whole of Scotland (so far - but we still have fifteen miles left!) He welcomed us in - pointed us in the direction of the showers and refused to take our money! What a great guy and what a beautiful place. I'm sitting with my feet in the Loch that we are camped beside as I type.

Hoping to manage the pain, I texted a friend at the beginning of the day, his brother is a doctor in the Lake District. I was hoping he might be able to help and perhaps pop over with a cortisone injection or something more appropriate, but early evening I got the reply that he wasn't able to help and I should go to Carlisle Hospital and get a specialist to look at it - yeh right! Oh well, plan B - keep going and see what else we can turn up.

One cheerful sponsor.

After a terrific steak à la Greg, we hobbled to the pub and got wi-fi, drinks and some friendly sponsorship from two great lads who had seen us on the service road earlier in the day. Strange pub, 3 TVs, all on, 1 juke box, also on, 2 slot machines, merrily singing their inane tunes, a pool table, just 12 locals and a barmaid. Little surprise I guess that no one commented on our slippers!

Today Scotland - tomorrow England, think I'll wear my Saint George socks again - as I did at the start...

PS. I've already finished my chocolate fingers (yes and I don't care) but John is still looking at the labels on his beers, funny man.

> **So - to the facts:** 360 miles run. Very big day tomorrow, completing our first mile of the day we have less than 500 miles to go and in about 15 miles it's the border at Gretna Green - now hands up and put £50 in the Cure Parkinson's box all those who thought we wouldn't make it - and yes I'm serious!

Session 1
9.68m 1:52.53

Session 2
19.85m 3:58.21

Session 3
29.94m 6:04.27

Marathon: 5:12.00

Mazzi
Can't believe anyone had doubts about the two of you finishing what you have started. Has John decided which beer to drink yet. Please tell him if they come home they are not allowed through the front door only in the garage!

Day 13 | **Lockerbie - St Cuthbert Without**

We've run a country

'The tragedy of life doesn't lie in not reaching your goal. The tragedy lies in having no goal to reach.'

Benjamin Mays

I kid you not

The barman/owner of the site had absolutely no knowledge of the whereabouts of St.Cuthbert Without. So not only are we not where the map says we are - we also have no idea what we are without!

As soon as we took our first step today the distance to go became less than 500 miles! 499 sounds so much better than 500, don't you think?

After six miles we passed through Ecclefechan (and yes we took a picture). The locals drop the Eccle (true) so as we ran through the town we passed the Fechan Library, then the Fechan Pub, the Fechan Police Station and finally the Fechan School. This has to be my favourite town of all time and I am starting a campaign to get it twinned with Peckham!

We took a short break after ten miles before heading for Gretna Green and the border. Greg let us down twice here. Firstly - much to our disappointment upon arrival at the Blacksmith's Forge, we discovered that he'd failed to publish our banns. So we elected just to have a photo but, no Greg. We spotted a couple nearby, Karen and John, so I asked if they would be kind enough to take a picture. It turned out they were returning to the Smithy to mark their 3rd wedding anniversary.

Just as we finished Greg turned up on his bike and took a photo - of THEM! After a brief chat he piloted us towards what can only be described as the least visual, tattiest border crossing in the world, not that it mattered in the least to us. 13 days, 375 miles and we have run a country!

The happy couple

We pressed on through Carlisle and just out the other side to our campsite. What a day - but it wasn't over yet. My wife, Sue, had searched the internet and found a sports physiotherapist who had experience of End to Enders. She not only understood my determination not to stop, but was also willing to drive out to our campsite after clinic hours to sort out my foot problems. Her name is Kathryn, but I've christened her the Angel of the North.

With her arrival imminent, I made my way as quickly as possible to the shower block. I hobbled into the shower, took my clothes off, fiddled with the controls for some time, but eventually gave up and put my clothes back on again. Leaving the cubicle I noticed a box on the wall that said showers 20p. So I hobbled back to the van, collected

5 May 2012

390 miles

20p and returned to the shower block. Noting a sign that warned the water would start as soon as the money was fed into the box. I slipped into the cubicle, removed my clothes once again then opened the door, enough to get my arm through, and slip the coin in. I swiftly shut and bolted the door, hopped (literally) into the shower and, just as promised, the water immediately started - in the cubicle next door! I got out of the shower as quickly as possible, put some clothes on, unbolted the door, and nipped into the next stall. Unsure now of how long I had before it stopped, I quickly soaped up and rinsed off in record time. So much for a relaxing shower at the end of a hard day. I got back to the van just in time to greet Kathryn.

We set her table up in the evening sun. In addition to making sure there is no fracture she worked the foot and calves and taped the foot so that it won't move in the wrong way when I run. In the full knowledge that I wasn't going to stop, her advice was to keep icing, elevating and walking the hills and all should be OK. What an angel - the Angel of the North.

So - to the facts: Never mind counties, we have now run a whole country! We have less that 500 miles to go, having run 390 miles and I am hopeful that with Kathryn's help, I may now have a chance.

Session 1
10.95m 2:12.38

Session 2
21.21m 4:15.24

Session 3
30.62m 6:17.13

Marathon: 5:18.38

Andy Tucker

Surely Fechan should be twinned with Hell? Aren't you glad you decided to run in the spring when the weather is so much nicer... You two knocking out 30 milers every day in this weather is a serious achievement. Still reckon you are as mad as a box of frogs.

Our Angel of the North

Day 14 — **St Cuthbert Without - Fawcett Forest**

Shap faced!

'I may not be there yet, but I'm closer than I was yesterday.'

Anon

SHAP HAPPENS! And it was quite a surprise for both us! Obviously we need a geography lesson - neither of us thought the highest climb of the run came before Kendal. Still, we made it and have the picture to prove it. For those still debating Land's End to John O'Groats or vice versa I think this little hill, and the direction in which it is tackled, should be taken into consideration (very happy to discuss).

We were very lucky with the weather today. It was cold and a little windy, but rain was forecast for our final leg of the day which included the 'Big Un'. The rain fell on our second break whilst we refuelled in the van - and as we walked up Shap the sun even came out. I must quickly add that it didn't make it any warmer - JT got brain freeze nearing the summit (1400ft) and had to hold onto his nose to prevent frostbite setting in. Being a few strides ahead I hadn't realised and was enjoying what I thought was a rousing rendition of Sgt Pepper's Lonely Hearts Club Band engineered to keep our spirits up. He agreed to let his defences down for just enough time to take a photo of us at the top by the memorial stone, then whizzed off down the hill leaving me in his wake.

Incidentally. The top of Shap has to be the most disappointing summit in the world, it's more like a Pylon Plantation.

It was a late finish, because my foot held us back, again. I set off this morning with renewed hope that pain was a thing of the past, big mistake. The first session was OK, but towards the end of the second session, it all came back into play, so we had to break the last section in two. Greg drove five miles up the road. We regrouped then he set off to within a mile of the summit, where we regrouped again before the final push. There was a short cut track we were going to use but we decided it was too rough and steep for us to safely use, so kept to the road. My leg really couldn't take any more today. It's like having a red hot knitting needle jabbed into the base of the shin every time I put weight on it while running and walking. Yesterday, I had hope, but today I'm left depressed. I feel as though I'm going to have to run all the way with this now.

It was 6.50pm by the time we made it to the campsite. There was little time for proper rest. We need to tighten up on time tomorrow to ensure an earlier finish. Shorten the breaks perhaps? Start slightly earlier?

6 May 2012

420 miles

On a more positive note, we met lots of end to end cyclists today and also had the pleasure of a brief chat with a chap walking the opposite way to us - Chris Hatton. He has lived in Porthcurnow, Cornwall, for two years and his wife said when they moved in, "one day you'll walk Land's End to John O'Groats". When he finally announced he was actually going to do it, she said - "about bloody time!" (I don't recall either of our wives saying anything remotely like that.)

> **So - the facts:** 420 miles down. Our second day in Cumbria. Tomorrow as we pass through Kendal, the end of our first section - we are Halfway - I think we can allow ourselves a small Woo hoo!

Session 1
10.22m 2:16.45

Session 2
19.29m 4:22.49

Session 3
30.20m 6:56.06

Marathon: 5:52.12

Preparing to go over the top

Sharon Gayter

Well done lads, you are doing amazing. Keep up the good work. Wanted to catch up with you this weekend, but never made it. I remember that hill well - stopped in Shap for an ice cream! Still watching with admiration for you.

49

Day 15 **Fawcett Forest - Lancaster**

Middle distance runners

Greg drove us to the start in his pyjamas this morning, which made a nice alternative to the van! He dropped us off at the foot of the second Shap climb, but it was only half a mile and then we enjoyed almost eight beautiful miles of predominantly down hill running into Kendal. Passing our caravan site about an hour and a half after we left. The inhabitants were about as interested in our passing as they had been in our presence the night before. What do you have to do to impress some people I wonder?

Kendal was beautiful, and full of runners taking part in the World Orienteering Championships. They wore all colours and ran in all directions. We blended in quite well with our bright yellow vests, water bottles and waterproof map case. We hope no one decided to try an easy ride and follow us!

The town is really charming. Between two lovely old bridges was the long awaited and hard worked for halfway point. We paused to congratulate one another and were just wondering how we could capture the moment when Amanda and Mike came along. We had a nice chat and they were very happy to take our photo at this historic point in our absurd adventure. Thanks Mike and Amanda - and thank you for the tweet. Great to meet you too!

Greg had left the van just outside Kendal to go off cycling around Lake Windermere, I think he found it more hilly than he expected. We were, of course, very sympathetic when we caught up at rest point two.

A few miles into the next session we met Zoe and her mum Colette, walking their dog in Milnthorpe. We stopped to chat while I noted down the phone number of an injury clinic!

It's a long long road, but we're gonna get there!

'Dropping out was a thought, but not really an option. For one thing, it made way too much sense.'

Mark Will-Weber

7 May 2012

450 miles

The end of section two was a disaster for me. I'd been going so well for eighteen and a half miles. Touching the ground very lightly and running on my toes, but with just over a mile to go all the bad stuff kicked in and I just couldn't manage the foot. The pain makes me feel quite nauseous at times. I raised and iced it when we reached the van, but was very concerned about the final ten so made lots of phone calls to see if we could organise a cortisone injection. I tried the hospital and therapy centres, but no joy. The hospital refused to help without a referral from a doctor. In response to a twitter from our Angel of the North a doctor did e-mail Greg to say he wouldn't give a cortisone unless I promised to rest for ten days!! Not much chance of a referral then.

We managed to finish off the day by splitting the section in two and taking a fifteen minute ice break in the middle. But the pain was so bad in the last four miles that the only way I could manage to finish was to speed up and keep counting to 100! Oh joy, roll on tomorrow...

So - the facts: Finished at 28.3 miles tonight because of the foot, but we had one mile in hand so are only 0.7 miles or so down. So, 20 miles over the halfway point at 450 miles. We also crossed another border today, from Cumbria into Lancashire.

JT wins mate of the day award for going the extra mile by popping into the local police station in the hope of finding a doctor to prescribe some pain relief. No luck, but what a mate!

The half-way point

Session 1
10.31m 2:12.39

Session 2
20.21m 4:24.15

Session 3
28.31m 5:59.40

Marathon: 5:34.08

Geoff
If you tackle the arctic next will you be able to combine ice treatments with running?

Day 16

Lancaster - Euxton

A little lift

'The mental will always master the physical, not only in athletics but in everything else as well.'

Arthur Newton

I kid you not...

I don't know if this independent fast food van also has pitches in New York, Paris, Peckham...

Only Food and Sauces

The answer is a packet of cigarettes! But more about that later. Now that's got you interested!

We met some fine characters today, all happy to sponsor the cause. In Lancaster we were stopped by Huw, who very kindly gave us £5 and offered us a cup of tea (which, sadly we had to turn down, the tea not the £5!) It was lovely to get such a warm greeting on what turned out to be a difficult start to the day. Cheered us up no end. Later, in Garstang, we met a most colourful fellow, Roderick Gilchrist, who had attended Millfield School as a boy and played rugby against my old school Dulwich College! I might also take this opportunity to pass on that Garstang is, apparently, the home of the Giant Onion. We didn't see it! It's also the world's first fairtrade town (I'm not completely sure how that works?!)

Whilst resting in a petrol station we met Rob Walker and his family who were also kind enough to fill JT's glove with coinage (don't ask). The desire to reach Land's End is matched only by our desire to reach £10,000 for The Cure Parkinson's Trust. In many ways the second is by far the hardest because it relies so little on our efforts, but the unfathomable generosity of others. We are tremendously grateful to everyone who has given us anything. If a million people give you a pound, you have a million pounds, as JT keeps saying.

The weather was very fair to us today - even the headwind wasn't bothersome. But I was concerned about the foot from the start, so in order to try and keep it going we reset the format of the day. We ran four sessions of seven miles, eight miles, eight miles and then another eight miles (because we were one short last night) and gave ourselves just a forty minute break between each. Running shorter sessions and icing in the breaks seems to have helped, along with some valuable advice we picked up from a chance meeting with a cyclist at the very start of the day. Paul saw we were End to Enders and stopped us to enquire how things were going. He was most concerned and suggested we pop in to see his podiatrist, just a mile down the road and on our route. With not a single physio returning our calls I was keen to make contact with someone, so we did just that. And what a good job we did.

8 May 2012

480 miles

A fruitful, early morning, chance meeting with cyclist Paul

I discovered that cortisone could certainly give me the relief I was seeking (good news), but at a serious price. The injection also weakens the tendon, which would almost certainly rule out four hundred more miles of running, which is what I needed to do (bad news). But it was good to be able to make an educated decision at last. As a practical alternative she suggested a heel lift, to take the pressure off the foot by reducing it's movement. This seemed, as she said, a far more practical answer, and one that Nick endorsed when he rang a little later in the day. We discussed the advice during our first break, and by our second break Greg had already made the purchase. I carefully popped it in my shoe before setting out on our last leg of the day. It immediately felt much much better, but it still wasn't quite right, it needed a little more support, so spotting an empty cigarette packet on the pavement I carefully folded it and slipped it in under the insole, and 'Hey presto!' Early days yet and tomorrow will confirm, but it felt as though it took the pressure off the painful area and allows me to run heel toe which has to be a good thing.

More good news was a lovely surprise, hiding in a Homebase carpark was an old clubmate, Steve Freemantle and his wife Sharron. Steve has driven all the way from Norfolk just to see us! That's a round trip of over 400 miles. We arranged to meet for a photo call with the ball at today's finish. I'm beginning to think the ball has more followers than us. We also arranged to meet up for a drink, without the ball!

> **So - the facts:** We finished tonight at 480 with just 380 miles to go. Off to Wigan tomorrow, Greg's looking forward to chips on the pier! Just 20 miles to the 500 - Woo Hoo!

Session 1
7.18m 1:32.14

Session 2
15.27m 3:05.15

Session 3
23.61m 4:41.22

Session 4
30.68m 6:03.53

Marathon: 5:12.20

Steve Forsdick

Nearly 500! That is a huge milestone! More than chips for that little celebration methinks. Looks like the foot is becoming the star of the show, maybe it should have its own blog?

Day 17 — **Euxton - Bartington**

A full day of meetings

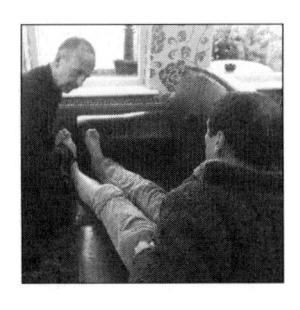

'Ability is what you are capable of doing. Motivation determines what you do. Attitude determines how well you do it.'

Lou Holtz

The day began with a farewell. Steve and Sharron were waiting for us in the carpark, which was our start this morning. A quick photo, lots of thankyous and we were off once again.

It seems to take around five miles to get the foot going, but after just two miles this morning we were both moving, almost, freely.

Not the best scenery England has to offer today, Wigan followed swiftly by Warrington! Highlight of the day was crossing the five hundred mile mark in the centre of Warrington. We took a picture of the most photogenic thing we could find which turned out to be us, and we've been running for 500 miles! And yes we did sing it.

Actually, the real highlight was meeting a young chap called Mark Keyes. It was just after Wigan in our first break of the day. It had just started to rain quite hard when we climbed into the van, and we were glad to be in the dry when we saw Mark heading northwards, carrying a huge backpack. We invite him in for a cup of tea and a sandwich. Turned out he is walking Land's End to John O'Groats in aid of Macmillan Cancer. He set off just two weeks after deciding to do it, with no real plan. Last night was the first night he had spent inside. His pack was almost too much for us to lift, but he was managing to walk fifteen to twenty miles a day. An inspiring young man with a great sense of adventure and spontaneity. I love this game, it's such fun and a great privilege to meet all these great characters and immediately feeling such a bond.

Break over, we donned wet weather gear, wished our new friend the very best of luck (especially through Glasgow) and headed off in the opposite direction. The rain stayed with us the rest of the day, all the way to the campsite, which we had elected to run a little over distance to.

We thought we were seeing double when we finally arrived. Greg had parked next to an identical motorhome. Also hired from Wild Horizon by a team of cyclists riding Land's End to John O'Groats!

We popped over to the local restaurant for something to eat and drink and met up with them in the bar. Greg had told them what we were up to so we were warmly invited to share a drink with them, Alan, Shaun, Elaine and John. Their encouragement and enthusiasm would have been enough after such a day but there was more to come. It turned

9 May 2012

510 miles

out that Alan's a Physio with his own practice in Streatham, just down the road from where I live. He was keen to have a look at my foot and offer some welcome advice. The last few miles had been quite tough on it, so it couldn't have been better timing. Sadly the answer to the problem remained the same - rest! Stop running! Hmmm, not really going to happen. Well not for another three hundred and fifty miles, then I'll think about it!

Conscious of how late it was getting and our need for food, we made our excuses and moved into the restaurant for a well earned steak dinner in a warm pub, as the rain (that Maz assures us is somewhere else) thundered on the glass roof. It wasn't just for us, we thought we owed Greg a night out, as he's feeling a bit under the weather and been stuck in the van all day, in the rain. (Did I mention it rained most of the day?) We do love 'im.

> **So - the facts:** This is getting serious - we've run over 500 miles! And we claimed another border, we are now in Cheshire.

Huge respect to our new friend Mark Keyes

Session 1
8.05m 1:38.57

Session 2
16.12m 3:13.37

Session 3
24.17m 4:52.20

Session 4
30.51m 6:09.46

Marathon: 5:13.48

Mazzi

So sorry for the wrong forecast only telling you what I heard on the BBC! Hope you enjoyed your meal. Glad they're treating you well, Greg.

Day 18 **Bartington - Quina Brook**

Royston Vasey?

No one could possibly have predicted how today would end! We started from the campsite today. Just thirty metres from the motorhome. We posed for a group photograph before waving goodbye to our new cyclist friends. We stood and watched them, as they headed off towards John O'Groats and what promised to be a very wet day. We then turned and headed off in the opposite direction, minus our jackets for only the second time in nearly three weeks.

There were no major conurbations to navigate today so we just relaxed into the road that took us due south towards Whitchurch where we were due to meet Simon Parsons - a Vice President of Blackheath & Bromley Harriers who now lives there and was keen to run part of the way with us.

We made good time today, but the running didn't come easy. By the time we met Simon, a couple of miles outside the town, my foot was struggling so, rather sadly, we had to walk most of the way to the van for our break - sorry Simon. It was a great pleasure catching up and sharing experiences while we refuelled. Break over, Simon generously escorted us, at our pace, out through what remained of the town and made sure we were on the right road for our final leg of the day before wishing us a warm farewell. We were keen to get to the campsite because JT's brother-in-law Lester and his wife (Lester's not John's) Chris were waiting to see us.

> 'Once you have established the goals you want and the price you're willing to pay, you can ignore the minor hurts, the opponent's pressure and the temporary failures.'
>
> **Vince Lombardi**

JT and fellow Club Vice President Simon Parsons

10 May 2012

540 miles

Our approach to the site should have made us suspicious. You know those feelings you get that really shouldn't be ignored? The road became a lane which then became a very narrow lane. The kind of narrow lane that suggested motorhomes don't come this way very often. When we arrived it was to a rather shabby farmhouse with a small concrete yard and a front lawn. The farmer asked us to park on the lawn, which we immediately did, we then immediately sank! With all hands on deck. Luckily (is that the right word?) the farmer had a tractor so he was able to tow us free (with only slight damage to the van) and then allowed us to park on the concrete yard! We were the only people there and I think probably were for the last twenty years, judging by the state of the toilet and shower, a small wooden hut, lifted on bricks that was accessed through a curtain of the farmer's mother's voluminous drawers. Towels like lumps of wood, soap grey and fractured, magazines no longer published... suffice to say nobody had a shower, or anything else!

The whole scene made us feel very uncomfortable and somewhat unsafe. And just to add to the atmosphere we had no phone or wi-fi connection, and it was now blowing a gale with torrential rain. JT was grateful for an opportunity to escape to a nice restaurant with Lester and Chris, but Greg and I thought it unwise to leave the motorhome unguarded. Yes it was that uncomfortable.

We gave JT a password and nervously waved him off, then settled down for a cosy lads night in with a couple of episodes of Top Gear to distract us. Life was almost normal! Apart from the mad farmer and his mother and a yard littered with massed weapons of painful destruction. Needless to say when JT returned, he'd forgotten the password!

During the night, all one could hear was eerie, whining, soulful singing coming from an upstairs, darkened room. Seriously worrying! Sometimes the important things in life are survival, not running!

> **So - the facts:** Most importantly, as at 10.06 pm, we are still alive. Not all Caravan & Camping Association sites are up to the same standard. 540 down 320 to go! And we are now in Shropshire.

Session 1
7:11m 1:25.04

Session 2
14.90m 3:00.31

Session 3
22.99m 4:43.50

Session 4
30.06m 6:15.51

Marathon: 5:26.01

Cliff Keen
I see this being made into a film in the future - who would you like to play you? Looking forward to the next dramatic scene.

Day 19 — Quina Brook - Marshbrook

Escape to the country

It was a very, very long night. I found it difficult to sleep, so the strange, whining, soulful singing coming from a dark upstairs window was a pleasant distraction. I'm really not sure who left the biggest impression. Them on us or us on them, their front lawn in particular. Either way we were more than keen to wave a fixed grin goodbye and be back on our way to normality, assuming that it's still out there somewhere.

So back out on the open road, doing what we do best with a huge sense of 'it's mighty good to be alive' in our step. The Shropshire scenery is beautiful. Georgous green rolling hills surround us. On our second leg of the day we ran through Shrewsbury - what a lovely old place. It's a shame we couldn't stay longer and take a few more photos, but our revised schedule means we have to press on so as not to finish too much after six o'clock. As we passed through the outskirts we met Peter Gill who was kind enough to sponsor us along with another couple, Martin and Lynn, who we met in the carpark where we took our second rest. So not only is Shrewsbury a wonderful place, it is filled with the most wonderful people - take a bow inhabitants of Shrewsbury!

'Every man is the architect of his own fortune.'

Sallust
86 BC – 35 BC

I kid you not...

A long way from Moon River but in a lay-by, how could one resist...

Breakfast at Timothy's

Small Batch Camp Site, Little Stretton

11 May 2012

570 miles

As we were getting ready to leave for our final leg there was a knock on the door - it was our Blackheath & Bromley Harriers AC friend Martyn Longstaff and his young grandson Mark. We were able to enjoy a brief chat before heading off up the A49 on our last section of the day. Martyn is hoping to come and run a few miles with us tomorrow.

The last section of the A49 was particularly difficult again. Fast cars and lorries with no room to pass, so we were forced to jump up and down off the high grass verges again. Not something I'm so good at now. It was a tremendous relief to finish. But although it's the end of the run for today, it's not the end of the A49. I will look closely at the map tonight and see if the road looks as bad for tomorrow or if there is a quieter (though usually more winding and hilly) route that will take us where we need to go.

The drive to the campsite was short and back the way we came, so there was no opportunity to see the road ahead for tomorrow. Turning off the main road we crossed a shallow, but fast flowing, ford to reach the site which nestled snuggly in the beautiful Shropshire Hills. Stopping us at the gate the warden suggested that we might like to take a walk as it was such a lovely evening! Hmmm.

It really is in the most delightful setting but quite basic, so there are no washing facilities for clothes, which means we now have three days of unwashed kit. I guess we could have asked at Royston Vasey last night!

On the bright side, and Eric says one should always look on the bright side of life, JT's wife Maz and her school friend Barbara and husband Mike are visiting tonight so we have arranged to meet them in the local pub. A welcome chance to get dressed up and put my slippers on.

> **So - the facts:** We finished on 570 tonight which means we now have only 290 miles to go. Oh and roads that end in a 9 are a pain in the...f**t

Session 1
7.59m 1:31.31

Session 2
14.55m 2:57.55

Session 3
23.17m 4:54.14

Session 4
28.92m 5:57.41

Marathon: 5:28.59

Richard Griffin
Not far now, you are both doing so well. Enjoy reading your Blog and seeing all your photos.

Day 20   **Marshbrook - Wellington Marsh**

Long running chums

What a wonderful evening with Maz, her friend Barbara and husband Mike (not Maz's husband Mike, Maz's husband is John, who has been running from John O'Groats to Land's End, which is an incredible coincidence because so have I! but Barbara's husband Mike. You remember Barbara she's Maz's friend!)

Suffice to say, we enjoyed a terrific meal with plenty of pudding and drink and Barbara's husband (not Maz's) Mike very kindly and most generously treated us all - he also paid for the dinner! Sincere thanks Mike. Note to those considering such an adventure, it's a terrific way to get free food and drink in restaurants and pubs!

One of the main advantages to staying in campsites is the ability to wash and dry our kit. With a change every break, and 2-3 layers of clothing in addition to jackets, there was quite a lot to do each night. Last night was the third night in a row that there had been no facilities, so as soon as he'd dropped us off at our start point, Greg fast forwarded to Craven Arms in order to find a launderette. When we arrived in town we ran right past him, because he had also managed to get himself a shorter than planned (not that we knew he even had a plan) haircut! We assured him it would grow back by the time he got home to Debs, with our fingers firmly crossed behind our backs.

It really was a glorious morning and it just got better. The sun shone, the A49 was nowhere near as bad as we thought it would be and our next stop, Ludlow, has to be the most lovely town in the country (so far). It was also 'Festival Weekend' (festival of what we never discovered, but it was obviously a happy festival because it was full of very happy people, which made a welcome change for us. We especially liked John, Hazel, Chris and Maggie who where particularly friendly (and happy) and made a donation to our cause. Which made us very happy.)

The tall one is Martyn!

'Life (and running) is not all about time but about our experiences along the way.'

Jen Rhines

I kid you not...

Ludlow has more Michelin Starred restaurants than any other town in the UK...

But we have Greg!

60

12 May 2012

600 miles

Terri taking a photo of the Three Amigos. The tall one in the middle is Mike!

As we climbed out of town we got beeped and waved at by a people carrier that then screeched to a halt a few hundred yards in front of us. As the dust settled, Martyn Longstaff appeared, in full Blackheath kit, all ready to run with us to our next break. It still amazes me that people are willing to associate, let alone run, with us! When we reached the van, about 4 miles further up the road, his daughter Vicki and 4 grandchildren, were waiting in the sunshine. It was wonderful to have another Harrier to run with and a real pleasure to meet the whole family.

Break over, we left Greg talking to a group of local cyclists, who were taking part in a time trial race from the lay-by we were parked in, and headed off into the sunshine once again. At our last stop of the day, in a lay-by just six miles from our campsite, we had just settled in the van when there was a loud knock on the door and Mike Peel climbed in, swiftly followed by Terri Shotton. They had been looking for us and pulled into the lay-by to consult the map and ended up nose to nose with our van! It was a complete surprise and so wonderful to see more clubmates. Mike 'just happened' to have his kit with him, so finished off the day by running to the campsite with us as Terri drove backwards and forwards stopping in lay-bys to take photos. What a great end to the day. And it got better because Mike and Terri have decided to stay at the bed and breakfast on our site and we are all going out for a meal tonight. I'm really getting to like this running lark. (I told you it was a great way to get free food!)

So - the facts: 600 miles run (so big celebration tonight) and only 260 to go. I know it's been said before but - Woo Hoo! Oh and we've crossed into Herefordshire.

Session 1
8.24m 1:38.38

Session 2
17.97m 3:26.02

Session 3
25.07m 4:46.43

Session 4
30.62m 5:50.36

Marathon: 4:54.28

Barbara and Mike Dunnett

It was great seeing you last night, glad you like Ludlow, we do too. Good luck for the next 260 - Barbara and Mike x

Day 21 — **Wellington Marsh - Llandogo**

Nicked!

Mike and Terri were there to wave us off this morning - which was wonderful. It makes a great start to the day.

It was a sluggish first section this morning, but navigating Hereford woke us up and after a rest we managed to get back into our rhythm and enjoyed the sunshine, scenery and hills.

Our club physio, Nick Nuttall, who offered to come down for a couple of days to help us out, met us on the road just before Monmouth. After a brief chat he headed off to find Greg, who had been back into Hereford for some sightseeing and then on out for a long cycle ride and was last seen heading for Monmouth. A short while later Nick came back towards us with Greg, and his bike on board. The next time we saw them was in the centre of Monmouth High Street. Greg and the van facing one way and Nick with his car facing the other, both looking quizzically at a one way street with a No Entry sign, that was the route to the bridge. We simply ran through the 'No Entry' sign to the bridge and out of town. I've no idea how they found their way out, but they eventually passed us and pulled into a lay-by a quarter of a mile ahead.

During our rest we met a fascinating couple of walkers, Waltraud and Barry. Waltraud impressed us greatly when she told us she had cycled to Munich and back on a tandem... Hmmmm now there's an idea. John - can you ride a bike? John? JOHN?

Post break, we enjoyed a delightful last six miles of rolling road through a canopy of trees, along the river Wye in the warm evening sun.

By some strange coincidence the 630 mile mark was right next to a pub garden. Funny that. Nick had the massage table all set up, but we had to wait our turn while he worked on the red ball, I'm beginning to think this ball is getting more attention than we are.

We enjoyed a very welcome drink in the evening light and a relaxing chat with a young couple, Darryl and Clair.

Following a careful bit of navigation down a very narrow road (and one wrong campsite) we arrived at our stop for the night, only to meet another End to Ender, who is walking with his two dogs, northwards. Yet another drunken bet. I should just like to point out that at no point in the planning of this adventure has alcohol played an influential part.

'Human beings are made up of flesh and blood, and a miracle fibre called courage.'

George Patton

13 May 2012

630 miles

And that no animals were harmed - well not by us anyway. (We have seen quite a lot of road kill - and just as an aside, I won't be buying Highland water from Sainsbury's in the future, because I know just how many deer and sheep there are in it!)

Nick stayed for dinner and then set up an impromptu massage room in the gent's toilet and showers. What a guy.

When I got back from my massage, JT was hosting an impromptu party of his own in the motorhome with two ladies and a baby. Erica and baby Rugi needed somewhere warm to shelter while Greg helped her husband, Simon, put up their yurt. And Valerie seemed very impressed with our efforts and came across to sponsor us, having already had a conversation with me in the gents. Every day, something new!

> **So - the facts:** 630 down 230 to go. Big day tomorrow - wind permitting we cross the Severn Bridge and turn right! I can hardly wait. If I wasn't so tired I'd be so excited I wouldn't sleep. But I am (tired that is) so I will... Today we passed through Monmouthshire and Gloucestershire.

Session 1
7.93m 1:37.43

Session 2
15.45m 3:20.37

Session 3
23.62m 5:02.37

Session 4
29.82m 6:08.31

Marathon: 5:30.40

Gerald
WOW, can't believe how far you have run in such a small amount of time!

Day 22   **Llandogo - Yanley**

A tale of two bridges

What a great, great day. We have finally crossed the Severn Bridge and turned right. What a moment. Hard to explain what it feels like to have reached this point. The picture is of 'The Right Turn!'

'The greatest pleasure in life is doing the things people say we cannot do...'

Walter Bagehot

The Severn Bridge came a mile into our second run. It was a long climb from the start, that took us past the stark ruins of Tintern Abbey. Followed by a long run down past Chepstow Racecourse (totally hidden behind an exceedingly high wall) to our first rest point at a roundabout on the outskirts of the town. I have to confess to being more than a little impatient to get out on the road again. We'd been dreaming about crossing the bridge and turning right since our last champagne moment, the Scottish Border. In the end, I managed to encourage JT out of the door five whole minutes early.

We stepped onto the bridge together. We could have run, but we felt that it was such a significant moment that we decided to indulge ourselves after so many miles and walk to the centre of the bridge. Huge waves of emotion swept over us. It was the point at which we began to feel that we were really going to make it now. When we reached the far side we paused at the roundabout to photograph the long awaited right turn. It might not look much to you, but to us it was everything!

There was surprisingly little wind on the bridge, but as soon as we were back in England and heading west, the wind blew strong and in our faces. We struggled for a while to the break then looked for an alternative route that was quieter, more sheltered and as it turned out, far more scenic, oh, and hilly (strange how all our alternative routes have involved more hills). Greg came out on his bike to guide us to the van as he'd tucked it down a side street beside Bristol Zoo. It's a shame we haven't had time for sightseeing but I've got quite a list of places that I would like to go back to now, and a mental note of quite a few I certainly don't want to (er... Glasgow!).

Farewell Wales...   *hello England*

14 May 2012

660 miles

Our final run of the day swept us down under the Clifton Suspension Bridge. What an amazing piece of inspired engineering. Following the bridge we had to do some really delicate navigation of some complicated major road intersections (with no pavement or hard shoulder) before we found ourselves on a much quieter country lane leading to Yanley. We were surprised to see Greg earlier than expected. The road we had arranged to meet on was apparently far too narrow for the van. As rain clouds were circling we readily agreed to stop a mile short. After all, we had champagne to open, and thanks to Nick's generosity a bath and massage in his hotel room just five minutes drive from our campsite - Woo hoo!

Our finish photo was with David Plester, a cyclist struggling with a flat tyre. He agreed to a group photo with the ball balanced on his bike for the loan of a pair of pliers! Which he then very hurriedly returned when his wife turned up with a pair from home, having driven eight miles through rush hour traffic!

The majestic span of the Clifton Suspension Bridge

Sadly, time was against us so I was unable to have a bath, just a quick shower before my massage. I had to listen to JT languishing in a warm bath while Nick worked on my quads and foot. Humph. But while we rested in the bar (I was more than tempted to use his bed!) Nick collected Greg so that we could enjoy dinner together overlooking the rather romantically floodlit suspension bridge. Thanks just isn't enough. Full marks Nick, but you do need a new satnav.

So - the facts: After 642 miles WE TURNED RIGHT! 660 miles down and just 200 to go. Nick Nuttall is a star.

Session 1
8.73m 1:53.09

Session 2
17.33m 3:36.59

Session 3
24.88m 5:18.00

Session 4
27.71m 5:55.17

Marathon: 5:38.17

Steve Hollingdale

Great stuff and still going strong. Entering scrumpy country now, followed by clotted cream with pasties not far away. Remember to stop at Land's End. Even though you may think you can walk on water by then...

Day 23 — Yanley - Bridgwater

Nothing like a short cut

'Never stop exploring. If you are not constantly pushing yourself, you are leading a numb existence.'

Dean Karnazes

We had a great time with Nick last night, being spoilt rotten. And his kindness continued in the morning, when he turned up at the campsite with hands full of pastries and croissants that he'd managed to smuggle from the breakfast buffet for us.

He drove with us to the start, determined to witness the point on our run when the distance remaining turned to less than 200 miles. (Greg never understood this game, but for some ultra runners it's an important part of the process and helps to retain a positive attitude.) Having shepherded us safely through to this point he waved a final farewell and left for home.

The next few miles were surprisingly hilly and slowed us down considerably. Always keen to revise the route when necessary, over breakfast, I found an obvious link between two roundabouts, a little further up the road, that for some reason I'd missed when I initially plotted the route. This road would cut off a significant loop and possibly save us a good half mile, maybe more. Eager to make up the time lost on the hills we pressed keenly on. Imagine our disappointment when upon closer inspection, it turned out to be the main runway of Bristol Airport! Not cleared for take off - we took the planned original route.

Greg, on the other hand, went one better. He parked up a little too close for comfort to our disguised 'short-cut' and got moved on by the police. Apparently, so the officer said, pilots in approaching aircraft had been radioing in! (Greg does have an awesome close up video of an easyJet plane landing if anyone's interested?! You might even be able to hear the pilot...)

We were incredibly blessed by a complete stranger today. When Greg filled up the van with diesel at the petrol station and went to pay, the previous customer had left £50 toward our fuel bill! Of course he'd driven off by now so there was no way to say thank you. What a terrific act of random kindness, it certainly kept us smiling for the rest of the day.

Inspired by all this generosity and the sunshine (and fuelled by Nick's croissants and pastries) we ran a long second leg which meant just two short legs to finish the day in the centre of Bridgwater, where we met two lovely elderly local gentlemen on their way to play a game of snooker. They each gave us a pound and kindly agreed to be

15 May 2012

690 miles

photographed with the ball for our final picture of the day. One of the things I will always remember about this adventure, will be all the wonderful people we have met, and would not have met had we not been out here on the road. Such a rich and valued experience.

We had a real sense of getting there today - and even began to work out at what time of day we might cross the line....no, no clues! Not yet anyway.

So - the facts: 690 miles run with just 170 miles to go. After ten miles tomorrow we have run 700 miles. After 20 miles we cross from Somerset (having run through North Somerset) into Devon.

It hardly seems possible.

Some caravan parks are more popular than others

Session 1
9.01m 2:01.22

Session 2
19.09m 3:57.51

Session 3
25.18m 5:06.42

Session 4
30.15m 5:58.14

Marathon: 5:16.38

John Leeson

Chaps fantastic effort, I can almost feel the aches and pains!! sitting in a comfortable chair drinking a nice cup of tea doesn't quite seem right. I guess Scones and Clotted cream will be provided by Nick shortly. Very best wishes.

67

Day 24 **Bridgwater - Tiverton**

A strange turn of events

'Some people dream of success... while others wake up and work hard at it.'

Anonymous

I kid you not...

I'm guessing this cleaning company van is driven by the boss...

Spruce Springclean

Song of the day...'Devon, we're in Devon!' It's an extraordinary feeling to think we've run all the way from Scotland to Devon. 710 miles to the county border. Our penultimate county, just one more to go.

It wasn't all plain sailing however. We did have a bit of an adventure along the way. We asked Greg to park the van at the eight mile mark just before Taunton. He gave us the key to let ourselves in so that he could go off for a cycle. A few miles into our run he texted us it's location. The sun shone, the birds sang, the miles swept by, and we missed the turn. We had looked at it carefully, but it wasn't signed as the map showed. Greg had also missed it first time around apparently, so he wasn't in the least bit surprised when we rang to tell him a little further on.

So we sailed on, only realising a mile further down the road, when it was too late to turn back. Never mind we thought we'll find a café and organise our own break. But all we ran past was a closed pub. Finally we found ourselves on the busy A38 dual carriage way through Taunton, having run nearly nine miles (a tad further than I really wanted for my foot). We worked our way along the rough verge for half a mile or so, until we spotted a 24hr Asda. We skipped carefully across two lanes of traffic, hurdled the central reservation, rather impressively I felt (I'm sure it's on camera somewhere!) and ran to the other side of the road. Our reward when we eventually found a way in, was real coffee, cold bottles of water, crisps and sandwiches all in the comfort of their café - oh, and a packet of peas for my foot! We also got sponsored - thanks Edward, Simon and friends! All together quite a treat. And with a bit of careful navigation to get us back on track, it cost us no extra distance. Result!

As the weather was holding, for our last run of the day, we decided to run an extra mile to make up the one we lost in Bristol because the van couldn't get down the road we were due to finish on.

JT Asda well earned break!

16 May 2012

720 miles

Our first glimpse of the van at the end of the third section

Fortunately the last mile sloped gently down, past the famous Blundell's Independent School, to our finish point on the outskirts of Tiverton where we met two lovely local runners, Michelle and Mary, who continued to keep in touch and followed our blog all the way to the end. Michelle was wearing a T-shirt for the Grizzly, which much to Greg's amusement, we said was far too difficult for us! Michelle said we should enter and she would personally escort us round. We'll get back to you on that one.

The campsite closed early, at eight o'clock, and doesn't approve of people going out - so it was another quiet night in! Sorry Greg.

> **So - the facts:** We finished tonight on 720 miles with 140 to go. We are now in Devon, our penultimate county. Thanks for all the encouragement folks - it's not getting any easier, but we are still enjoying ourselves tremendously!

Session 1
9.36m 1:55.18

Session 2
15.78m 3:18.54

Session 3
23.48m 4:54.26

Session 4
30.83m 6:23.35

Marathon: 5:23.34

Chris Pike

Go easy on the clotted cream chaps...don't want too much excess baggage with you up those hills....Can hardly believe you are so close to the end...what will you do for an encore? Brilliant job chaps.... woohoo!!!!

69

Day 25 — **Tiverton - Okehampton**

In history's footsteps

'Running is a mental sport...and we're all insane!'

Anonymous

Tomo

Tom...oh! Much discussion has taken place about the legendary bagpiping 'heathen called Dave Thomson. Is it Tomo, Tommo or Thomo. We have used 'Tomo' in this tome, and regardless of people's preferences we can confirm that, as football supporters sing, "there is only one Tomo" (or Thomo or Tommo!).

The day began well with JT collecting a generous donation from a lovely couple on the caravan site - Dewi and Iona. A very welcome and unexpected start to the day.

And at the start, another welcome surprise was waiting for us. An elderly couple, standing at their gate, saw us finish last night and were interested to hear our story. They were bubbling over with good questions. They remembered meeting Dr. Barbara Moore when she walked from John O'Groats to Land's End in just 23 days. It was her walk, in 1960, that kick-started the modern End to End boom. A precious moment for us to talk about, and touch, a little piece of history. It certainly fuelled us with a little extra energy for the start of our day 25 (we tried not to dwell on the fact she completed it in 23 days and we still have the best part of a week to go!)

It might have been an inspired start, but within 5 miles the rolling hills of Devon kicked in and kept us company all day.

Greg had a lovely day out on his bike. We kept meeting him every time we were leaving the van. The picture is Greg suffering for his art. He wanted to take a photo from the field, but it involved hopping over a barbed wire fence. Don't worry Debs he should be back to normal by the time you see him! (Have received no confirmation yet .ed)

Our friend and clubmate Tomo rang during our final run to finalise arrangements for 'piping' us into our last county. We should enter Cornwall at about 3.00 tomorrow afternoon - to the sound of the bagpipes! Now that's a photo worth waiting for.

The picture for which Greg risked it all

17 May 2012

750 miles

Magic moment of the day... it's raining and JT and I were walking up a twisting country road, map in hand... a young man in a tipper truck slows beside us, winds down his window and most generously asks if we'd like a lift. "No thanks mate", we answered cheerfully in unison, "we've only got another 120 miles to go!" The expression on the man's face was absolutely priceless! No further words were exchanged and he continued on his way. We had to chuckle, we keep forgetting that we're just not normal!

We are getting so close now, and our bodies are beginning to let us know. We are in high spirits, but each day seems a little longer as it absorbs more effort. And the rolling hills offer very few flats that allow us to get into any kind of rhythm. Having said that, we are still very glad that we have chosen to run it this way round. As the thought of a four day finish on the A9 is - er unthinkable!

> **So - the facts:** We finished today on 750 miles with 110 to go. So 11 miles into our run tomorrow we have less than 100 miles to the finish. And in 20 miles we leave Devon and enter Cornwall, our last county. We are so nearly there. It hardly seems possible.

"We're only bloody doing it!"

Session 1
7.87m 1:43.51

Session 2
15.87m 3:24.41

Session 3
24.09m 4:58.00

Session 4
29.91m 6:10.15

Marathon: 5:24.30

Bernie
Greg looks like a decent hurdler to me! Well done boys not long now!

Day 26   **Okehampton - St Ive**

The ultimate border crossing

> 'It's at the borders of pain and suffering that the men are separated from the boys.'
>
> **Emil Zatopek**

I kid you not...

After 764.2 miles of steady running - JT fell over! (Don't tell Maz.)

What a truly memorable day! Tomo we salute you! You are a first class gent and they broke the mould when they made you.

A tricky start to the day with a mad dash up the A30. A very busy dual carriageway, with fast moving traffic and no hard shoulder. Fortunately only one junction and only one mile. Thank goodness we haven't chosen this as our route all the way to Land's End.

Back on the quiet road we were hailed by a chap sitting on a gate. Jim Cole, an athletic young man with a 1:09 half-marathon time. He was concerned we were lost when he saw us carrying a map. After a brief chat he was kind enough to confirm we were running the shortest route to Tavistock.

The road took us up and over the western edge of Dartmoor. We were glad the wind was behind and the weather fair. Visibility was not good, but it was beautiful all the same, and it felt like something of an achievement to be crossing the moor. After a long, gradual climb, it was a welcome long run down to our first rest of the day, just four miles before our final border crossing, and a long awaited appointment with Tomo.

Through Tavistock and up and over some steep hills and then, as we worked our way down a quad bashing country lane, we heard the unmistakable sound of the pipes. We ran out of the woods and onto an old stone bridge across the Tamar where Tomo stood, plum in the middle, resplendent in full Scottish regalia, playing The Grand Old Duke of York on the bagpipes to welcome us into Cornwall. What a sight, what a sound, and what an experience - after 770 miles! We posed for pictures and then arranged to meet at a pub a short distance further up the hill, for an unscheduled break.

In the car park we met Chris, who taught us how to pronounce St Ive - that'll be St Eve then! Our stop for the night. Inside the pub we met Hilary and Nikki who very generously made a donation. Turned out Hilary's husband had cycled End to End several times - including once on a Chopper bike! It takes all sorts!

A celebratory drink and a packet of crisps with Tomo in the pub and he piped us on our way again. He even piped Greg and the van off! Tomo you are one in a million and we will never forget our entry into Cornwall.

A moment and a day to remember, forever. Thank you Tomo

I would like to say that it feels down hill all the way now (as many well wishers have encouraged us), but in reality it is the exact opposite. Hills, hills, hills now we fear, and the downs are just as painful as the ascents. Onwards and upwards as they say!

So - the facts: 780 miles run. After 770 miles we've entered our last county - and what an entrance!!

18 May 2012

780 miles

Session 1
7:57m 1:38.05

Session 2
15.61m 3:10.59

Session 3
25.99m 5:08.29

Session 4
30.01m 6:07.00

Marathon: 5:11.29

Bernie
I dare you to blow the flame out tomorrow as it goes the other way. Keep going boys!

Day 27

St Ive - Grampound

Light entertainment

'Good things come slow - especially in distance running.'

Bill Dellinger

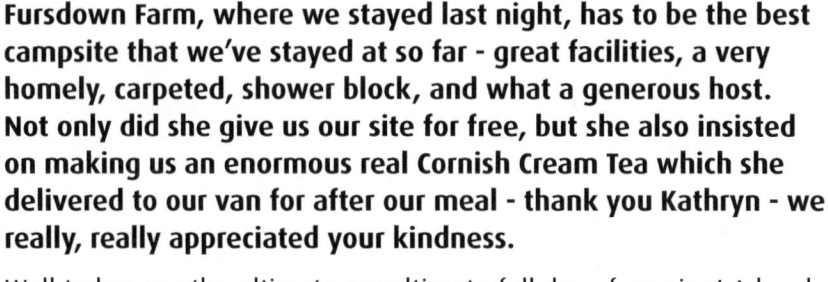

Fursdown Farm, where we stayed last night, has to be the best campsite that we've stayed at so far - great facilities, a very homely, carpeted, shower block, and what a generous host. Not only did she give us our site for free, but she also insisted on making us an enormous real Cornish Cream Tea which she delivered to our van for after our meal - thank you Kathryn - we really, really appreciated your kindness.

Well today was the ultimate penultimate full day of running! A lovely warm day that allowed us to run without the extra layers. We chose a quiet route away from the traffic to start, it was beautiful, but exceptionally hilly and we ended up having to walk the steep downs as well, sideways at times! We did however meet a couple of runners from East Cornwall Harriers, Tracy and Sam, who were out training for their first marathon. They seemed quite happy to spend a few minutes chatting. It was certainly a nice break for us before tackling the next hill.

The weather was so good that in our second break, we were able to get the folding canvas chairs out and sit on the grass for the first time! It was quite hard to leave them, but our sacrifice was rewarded very quickly. Just half a mile further up the road, as we crested the hill, we saw the South Coast. A surprisingly emotional sight. Difficult to understand, perhaps, unless you've run nearly 800 miles from the North Coast of Scotland. Not the most picturesque view but a precious photo to treasure just the same.

Earlier in the day the Olympic Torch relay had started at Land's End. It's planned route zig-zagged across Cornwall throughout the day. Tomo had rung us earlier to report that by Falmouth (where he lives) it was already an hour behind schedule. At this rate, I calculated, there was little chance it would turn up at the Olympic Stadium until a week after the games had started! Our schedule for the day didn't give us much hope of seeing it, although we did run through a few towns with crowds already gathering to greet it. But as we reached the outskirts of St Austell a cavalcade of Police motorcyclists, blue lights flashing, approached us. Realizing it must be the torch on its way to the next town we stopped and I got my phone out to take a picture. I waited for the best shot of the buses when it rang, diverting my phone from

19 May 2012

810 miles

camera mode! It was Greg to say he'd been watching the Torch Relay in the Town Centre and it was on its way! Thanks Greg - I just had to hope he got better pics than I did. As it turns out, he did, a lot better.

Another terrific surprise, was Tomo at the finish once again. We heard the pipes as we descended the last hill, and then there he was - with the red ball between his knees! We couldn't help laughing as we took our last few steps of the day. He followed us back to our campsite, where we all tucked into 'the best pasties in Cornwall' - generously provided by Tomo, of course. What a man.

So - the facts: 810 miles run with just 50 to go. We can hardly believe it. Tomorrow is our last full day of running. The end is in sight - almost literally...

Session 1
8.94m 2:15.04

Session 2
17.41m 4:10.14

Session 3
24.47m 5:43.54

Session 4
30.09m 6:56.56

Marathon: 6:11.03

Barbara & Michael

Nearly there - bet you won't sleep much tonight thinking of all you have done, all the places you have run through, all the wonderful people you have met. Good luck for tomorrow, we'll be thinking of you - you deserve to pig out on Cornish pasties & cream teas!

OF COURSE IT ALL STARTED WITH I MET THE JOGLE BROTHERS, PETE AND JOHN. THEY ARE THE REAL INSPIRATION FOR THIS JOURNEY. I MEAN WE'RE NOT GOING ALL THE WAY TO JOHN O'GROATS.

Day 28 Grampound - Ashton

A day of surprises

A lovely and unexpected start to the day - during our first run, we met Rob Wing with his beautiful Traction Engine, in full steam, about to pull out of a lay-by. He stopped for a chat and to allow us to take a photo. My brother Malcolm owns a Sentinel Steam lorry, the 'Shrewsbury Knave', which he drove from John O'Groats to Land's End, with eleven similar vehicles, in 1999. We are now very close to achieving the same, but under our own steam!! Ironically, and totally unplanned, we are due to finish on the same day that my brother did - May 21st.

The second stage was very difficult because of long hills and heavy, fast moving traffic. We were both quite tired by the time we pulled into our rest stop, but soon revived by the irrepressible Tomo, who turned up, cheery as ever, minus bagpipes but with three punnets of fresh Cornish strawberries and cream! What a man!

It was certainly a day for surprises. Greg had parked the van in a garage and gone for a long cycle, so we were left to look after ourselves at our

'Dreamers are not people disconnected from reality. Dreamers are people fully connected to reality's potential.'

Anonymous

Full steam ahead for Bob Wing

20 May 2012

840 miles

third break. We had only been in a few minutes when we were surprised by a polite knock on the door - it was JT's wife Maz and our running friend, from Dulwich, Helen - with Eccles cakes and Cappuccino coffees! It's obviously a day for surprise food and friends! How we missed seeing them as we approached the van, I have absolutely no idea.

Helen and Maz are booked into a youth hostel near Sennen Cove, around 20 miles further on. So while we headed off on the last leg of our last full day of running, they headed off to book-in to their accommodation, before returning later for dinner. Our last run of the day included two diversions onto much quieter roads that wound through farmland and small villages. The country lanes and lovely late afternoon sun, gave us a welcome opportunity to chat and reflect upon the challenge and to focus on our final day tomorrow.

At some point during today we were rather hoping to find our first signpost for Land's End, but in sight of the van, with almost thirty-one miles run, there was still no sign. Unusually, Greg indicated the point to which we should run and clock off for the day - an old mile-stone, Land's End 17 miles! It had to be the final photo of the day!

The campsite is lovely, just a short walk from the beach (too much for us!) and the owner Catherine very kindly gave us a cheque for The Cure Parkinson's Trust.

Maz and Helen picked the three of us up in the car and drove us to a pub that not only had everything we ordered on the menu, but served the best steak I have ever eaten, surpassing a steak I thought impossible to beat, at The Ritz Hotel, Piccadilly, in 1983. Much to the table's annoyance I have to confess to playing my Wobble on the Jogle Card tonight. Well the team deserved it!

Safely delivered back to our campsite we retired to bed, not expecting to get much sleep. We'll see.

> **So - the facts.** 840 miles run. Just 20 miles (or 17 if the old signpost is to be believed) to go! This isn't an exact science, but hills, weather and feet willing we still hope to finish around 3.00 pm tomorrow.

Session 1
8.26m 1:48.23

Session 2
15.83m 3:40.38

Session 3
22.75m 5:03.14

Session 4
30.78m 6:50.10

Marathon: 5:49.10

Steve Forsdick

It has been amazing reading this blog, I have enjoyed every word and every step, Enjoy tomorrow, what you are about to finish is just awesome, you are incredibly inspiring!

Day 29

Ashton - Land's End

We've only bloody done it!

'The miracle isn't that I finished. The miracle is that I had the courage to start.'

John Bingham

The Chairman
Blackheath & Bromley Harriers AC

Well done lads. You did us proud... not to mention yourselves! Enjoy the moment!

No words can adequately describe how it feels to finish such a challenge. We crossed the line at 2.06pm and it was a tie...for second place. Greg was the worthy winner, arriving at the finish a good thirty minutes ahead of us.

We left this morning with approximately eighteen miles to go. Our first stop was in Penzance where Greg had found a barber to cut JT's hair. A couple of weeks ago we were secretly sponsored £50 if JT finished minus his beard! As if running John O'Groats to Land's End wasn't enough! Leah was lovely, and did a great job, she refused to charge us and as well as allowing us to use her shop as a makeshift motorhome, topped up our water bottles before we left. We also picked up a contribution to The Cure Parkinson's Trust from one of her customers, Terry, who said he had seen our van near Bristol!

During our second session Tomo (who was now racing to reach Land's End before us) caught us up and then stopped in every lay-by to pipe us onwards to the finish. They really did break the mould when they made Tomo, our most enthusiastic (and loudest!) supporter.

Our last break was in a lay-by just four miles from the end. Time to gather our thoughts, eat a little, change and prepare ourselves for our final run. Greg drove ahead to the finish and JT and I set off for the last time. With blue sky, warm sunshine and just a slight breeze to cool us - we could not have asked for a more perfect day. We covered the last four miles in just 34:47. Much swifter than anticipated, but fuelled by a sense that we were so close to completing the challenge that had appeared almost insurmountable before the start. The road that leads to Land's End is far more picturesque than the A9 approach to John O'Groats and also inspired a turn of speed. And as the land narrows you can see the sea, glistening, on either side, such a beautiful way to finish. With two miles to go I rang my mother (the inspiration for this run) so that she should be a part of the final mile.

The road finally bends to the right and Land's End comes into view, it wasn't long before we heard the, now familiar, pipes and saw the finish - with Greg, Maz, Helen, and of course Tomo, standing on the finish line with his foot on the red ball. We jumped the line together - with the shout - 'We've only bloody done it!'

Warm hugs, from friends and a few bemused tourists, and cold champagne immediately flowed. I thought we'd drink the champagne but Greg had

21 May 2012

860? miles

L-R: JT, Maz, Tomo, Peter & Greg mid celebration!

other ideas, I'm so glad I asked him to put it in the fridge this morning. It certainly cooled us down after the run!! We posed for pictures on the line and drank what remained of the bottle before heading for the signpost and our official finish photograph.

Job done we enjoyed a wonderful champagne, strawberry and pasty picnic in the sunshine, overlooking the sea. Before leaving JT, Greg and I wandered up to the hotel to sign the End to End book and get the final stamp for our official membership of the End to End Club (certificate to follow!)

After a short rest and tidy up back at the campsite we enjoyed a well earned meal and slightly more than a few glasses in the 'First and Last Pub'. The ceiling is covered with signed vests of people who have run or walked the distance and they kindly agreed to put one of ours up as a permanent record of our achievement and more importantly, a permanent advertisement for The Cure Parkinson's Trust. Thanks guys.

We ate and drank until the pub closed and we were the only ones left in the bar. Then gentlemen that we are, JT and I walked(?) the ladies home to their hostel and then somewhat unsteadily retraced our steps under a canopy of a thousand stars, so bright you could almost reach out and touch them. Arm in arm we did our best to follow the white line down the centre of the road...

> **So - the final facts:** 854.8 miles in 28 days, 4 hours and 54 minutes.
> A total running time of 175 hours 3 minutes and 23 seconds.
> Total height gained and lost equal to three times up and down Everest.
>
> Fellow 'heathens we challenge you!
>
> Greg is claiming the record for the slowest drive from John O'Groats to Land's End in a motorhome - to be ratified...

Session 1
7.25m 1:15.51

Session 2
13.52m 2:37.21

Session 3
17.21m 3:12.08

Cliff Keen

Congratulations chaps, all three of you, what a team! It feels like we've been able to travel every step with you - exhausting, I shall need a lie down now that it is all over. Fantastic achievement, something for your, and BBHAC's, record books. Enjoy the Cornish beers, and being immobile for a while.

80

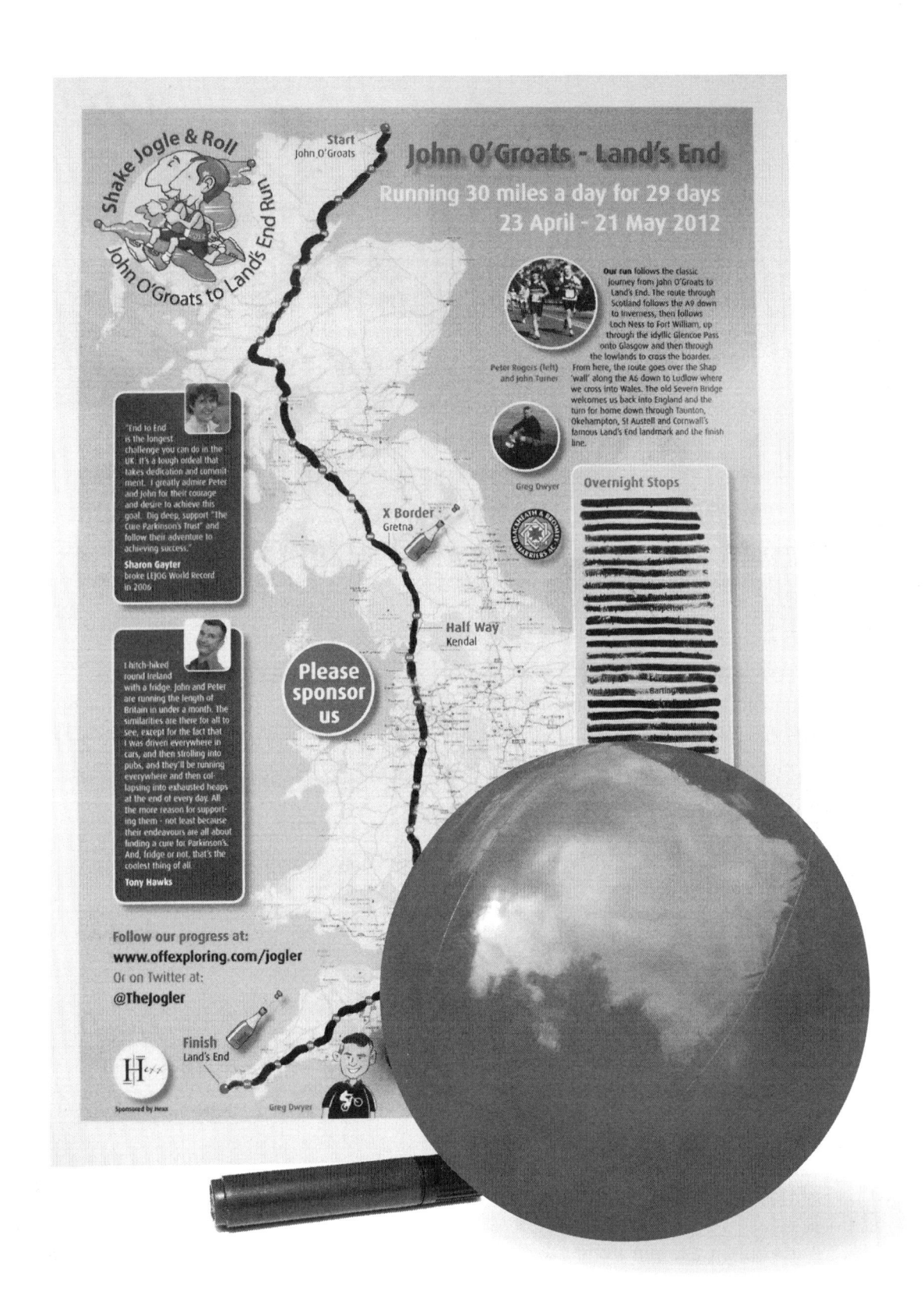

Hi Peter and John

I am so pleased for you. It is hard to put into words what it feels like to complete such a challenge, only those that have really conquered the distance understand this. So very well done on joining this great elite group, you did amazingly well and I was disappointed not to be able to catch up with you.

It is an almighty challenge that you set yourselves and I know it's a daily fight to complete it.

Recover well and this will live with you forever.

Thanks for inviting me to follow your journey, very proud for you.

Sharon Gayn

Training for the big one

Although the narrative of this adventure began when we left London, the story obviously began much earlier with the training.

We both started with a very strong endurance base. In 2011 I ran seventeen marathons (including my 100th), meaning a week's recovery running then a two week build to the next one. This has been our general running lifestyle for a good number of years and means either of us could (and sometimes have) run a marathon at almost a moment's notice. The focus for our training for this event was on how to run twenty-nine in a row without breaking down. This meant looking at sustainable pace, ongoing rest and nutrition on the run.

Running my 100th Marathon with JT and my youngest son Maff (his first) in April 2011

Very early on we decided that the most sustainable way for us to cover 30 miles a day was what became known to us as 2-1-2-1-2. Two hours running, one hours rest, two hours running, one hours rest, two hours running or less to finish the daily distance. So this is what we trained to do.

I tried my first 2-1-2-1-2 thirty mile run in Friesland (Netherlands) during my summer holiday. With Sue riding beside me on her bike carrying food and water. I was pleased to discover it worked very well. Almost as pleased as Sue was to discover she could ride thirty miles so well! At each break I had a sandwich, coffee or bouillon soup and a few crisps. I also enjoyed the odd biscuit at comfort breaks. Eating and running was not something I had much experience of. In ultras I find my stomach begins to close down after 6 hours or so, so I've only really nibbled bits of cake or my famous pick-me-up (guaranteed to get me going) chocolate raisins. I don't remember eating much at all in the second half of the 24hr track race.

The first 30 mile training run, in Friesland, July 2011

A few days later I tried it again and was just as pleased with the result. Although I don't recommend Crème of Asparagus Soup. The running time for the thirty mile distance for both runs was sub five hours. An early indication that the theory worked.

Back home and running together, we saved our long runs for the weekends when we ran a minimum of 2-1-1 but usually 2-1-2 building to 2-1-2-1-2 then eventually 2-1-2-1-2 for three days in a row over the Easter weekend. During the week our shortest run (our recovery) was never less than one hour and our normal three runs not less than two hours. The highest mileage week was 138 miles.

My usual solo two hour run was from home up to and across Tower Bridge, left in front of the Tower of London and along the north bank of the Thames, past St Paul's to Westminster Bridge. Once over the bridge it was then left along the South Bank, past the London Eye, National Theatre, OXO Tower, Tate Modern, the Globe Theatre, The Clink, The Golden Hind, Southwark Cathedral, HMS Belfast, the Mayor's office and finally back to Tower Bridge. Then retrace my steps through Bermondsey, across the Old Kent Road and into Burgess Park before chasing the old Surrey Canal back into Peckham and the final mile home. It's my favourite run and always gives me energy, especially in the early morning, when there are fewer tourists and the river is still and London is quiet.

It wasn't always easy to fit our long runs in every weekend as the blog for Saturday 24th March illustrated:

'This is not about instant gratification. You have to work hard for it, sweat for it, give up sleeping in on Sunday mornings.'

Lauren Fessenden

The training plan said '30 miles' for today. So...we ran from the Blackheath and Bromley Harriers AC clubhouse at 10.40am and arrived back at 12.44pm. Did a quick change into club kit (swallowed a coffee, ate a sandwich) and slipped into the Club Photo (which only happens once every four years - in Olympic year). 10 mins later at 1.44pm we headed out for the next 2 hour section while the rest of the club ran the club 5 mile X-country handicap at 2.30pm. We returned to the club at 3.45 in time to join in the 'Closing 5' tea and be presented with a charity cheque for £500 from our friend Ponti on behalf of the Master and Wardens of the Worshipful Company of Armourers & Brasiers (for which we are very, very grateful). We then headed out the door again - leaving our clubmates munching their cakes and tea - to run the last 5 miles to complete the 30. We sped through the five to finish in an overall running time of 4.54.09. Did I mention that it was full sun and hot all day? We arrived back at the clubhouse just 40 minutes before the AGM. I think the real thing is going to be an awful lot easier!!!

'Any idiot can train himself into the ground; the trick is working in training to get gradually stronger.'

Keith Brantly

The initial plan was to cover ten miles in each two hour section, a fairly pedestrian 12 minute mile pace. In practice we averaged a distance of twelve and a half miles leaving us just five or six miles for the last section which we could cover in an hour. Running time 5 hours, and therefore a running day of seven hours. Training at this level gave us plenty of scope for flexibility during the run itself when we allowed ourselves an eight hour day. Giving us a full 16 hours of rest a day.

The mid run rest breaks were just as important to rehearse. Eating and drinking in the first 20 minutes gave us 40 minutes to allow sufficient digestion before running again. After some experimentation I settled on a peanut butter and jam sandwich, coffee or broth, a few chocolate raisins, a packet of crisps, a banana and water. We were surprised how easy it was to get going again after these breaks.

During our training we were constantly being asked 'how do you train to run more than a marathon a day for twenty nine days?' The answer, 'two hours at a time.' Our philosophy for training has always been to do the least to gain the most. In other words, to do enough training for the event but not to risk over training and injury. Better to get to the start confident and raring to go rather than nursing a niggle or worse an injury.

Spot the two trainee Jogle runners in this club photo, taken at 1.34pm on the 24th March 2012

www.tomphillipsphotos.co.uk

Training plan - last three months

Mid-week (this was the basic plan but we often ran 6-12 miles on a rest day)   **Mid-week miles**

Mon	Rest	-
Tues	2hrs	12.5 miles
Wed	2hrs	12.5 miles
Thu	1hr	6.5 miles
Fri	Rest	-

30-45 miles

February | | | | **Total miles**

Sat 4	2-1-2	24.12 miles	3:53.6	
Sun 5				**55.62 miles**
Sat 11	1 hr	7 miles		
Sun 12	2-1-2-1-2	30 miles	4:54.18	**68.5 miles**
Sat 18				
Sun 19	2.5hrs	15 miles		**74 miles**
Sat 25	1 hr	7 miles		
Sun 26	2.5 hrs	15 miles		**53.5 miles**

March

Sat 3	2 hrs	12.5		
Sun 4				**72 miles**
Sat 10	2-1-2	24.25 miles	4:1.37	
Sun 11	2hrs	12.72 miles		**68.47 miles**
Sat 17	2-1-2	23.58 miles	4:6.41	
Sun 18	2-1-1	18.13 miles	3: 2.35	**110 miles**
Sat 24	2-1-2-1-2	30 miles	4:54.9	
Sun 25	2.5 hrs	15.62 miles		**77.12 miles**
Sat 31	2 hrs	12.5		
Sun 1	2-1-2	23.6		**67.6 miles**

April

Fri 6	2-1-2-1-2	30 miles	5:7	
Sat 7	2-1-2-1-2	30 miles	4:58	
Sun 8	2-1-2-1-2	30 miles	5:7	**138 miles**
Sat 14	2hrs	12.5		
Sun 15	2hrs	12.5		**56.5 miles**

> 'If you under-train, you may not finish, but if you over-train, you may not start.'
>
> **Stan Jensen**

Route and schedule

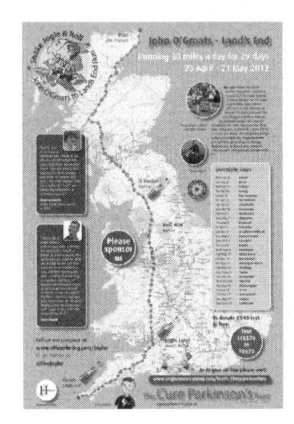

'Success is the sum of small efforts, repeated day in and day out.'

Robert Collier

Sa/Su April 21-22	Drive from London to John O'Groats		
Mon Apr 23	30 miles	30 miles	Latheronwheel
Tue Apr 24	30 miles	60 miles	Golspie
Wed Apr 25	30 miles	90 miles	Pitmaduth
Thu Apr 26	30 miles	120 miles	Beauly
Fri Apr 27	30 miles	150 miles	Fort Augustus
Sat Apr 28	30 miles	180 miles	Fort William
Sun Apr 29	30 miles	210 miles	Altnafeadh
Mon Apr 30	30 miles	240 miles	Inverarnan
Tue May 1	30 miles	270 miles	Dumbarton
Wed May 2	30 miles	300 miles	Chapelton
Thu May 3	30 miles	330 miles	Crawford
Fri May 4	30 miles	360 miles	Lockerbie
Sat May 5	30 miles	390 miles	St Cuthbert Without
Sun May 6	30 miles	420 miles	Fawcett Forest
Mon May 7	30 miles	450 miles	Lancaster
Tue May 8	30 miles	480 miles	Euxton
Wed May 9	30 miles	510 miles	Bartington
Thu May 10	30 miles	540 miles	Quina Brook
Fri May 11	30 miles	570 miles	Marshbrook
Sat May 12	30 miles	600 miles	Wellington Marsh
Sun May 13	30 miles	630 miles	Llandogo
Mon May 14	30 miles	660 miles	Long Ashton
Tue May 15	30 miles	690 miles	Bridgwater
Wed May 16	30 miles	720 miles	Tiverton
Thu May 17	30 miles	750 miles	Okehampton
Fri May 18	30 miles	780 miles	St Ive
Sat May 19	30 miles	810 miles	Grampound
Sun May 20	30 miles	840 miles	Ashton
Mon May 21	20 miles	860 miles	Land's End
Tue May 22	Drive from Land's End back to London		

Actual statistics

Day	Actual miles run	Running time	
Mon Apr 23	30.05 miles	5:08.35	Latheronwheel
Tue Apr 24	31.78 miles	5:47.23	Golspie
Wed Apr 25	27.45 miles	4:40.07	Pitmaduth
Thu Apr 26	29.79 miles	5:04.42	Beauly
Fri Apr 27	31.00 miles	5:50.53	Fort Augustus
Sat Apr 28	30.07 miles	5:23.57	Fort William
Sun Apr 29	29.43 miles	5:44.06	Altnafeadh
Mon Apr 30	30.07 miles	5:23.26	Inverarnan
Tue May 1	28.14 miles	5:49.58	Dumbarton
Wed May 2	30.56 miles	9:49.39	Chapelton
Thu May 3	30.09 miles	7:03.18	Crawford
Fri May 4	29.94 miles	6:04.27	Lockerbie
Sat May 5	30.62 miles	6:17.13	St Cuthbert Without
Sun May 6	30.20 miles	6:56.06	Fawcett Forest
Mon May 7	28.31 miles	5:59.40	Lancaster
Tue May 8	30.68 miles	6:03.53	Euxton
Wed May 9	30.51 miles	6:09.46	Bartington
Thu May 10	30.06 miles	6:15.51	Quina Brook
Fri May 11	28.92 miles	5:57.41	Marshbrook
Sat May 12	30.62 miles	5:50.36	Wellington Marsh
Sun May 13	29.82 miles	6:08.31	Llandogo
Mon May 14	27.71 miles	5:55.17	Long Ashton
Tue May 15	30.15 miles	5:58.14	Bridgwater
Wed May 16	30.83 miles	6:23.35	Tiverton
Thu May 17	29.91 miles	6:10.15	Okehampton
Fri May 18	30.01 miles	6:07.00	St Ive
Sat May 19	30.09 miles	6:56.56	Grampound
Sun May 20	30.78 miles	6:50.10	Ashton
Mon May 21	17.21 miles	3:12.08	Land's End
Total	**854.8 miles**	**175:3.23**	**28d 4hr 54min**

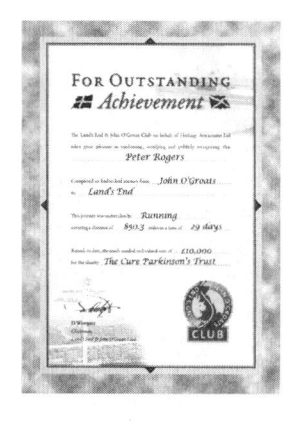

Take our total time (175:3.23) and divide it by the number of days we ran (29) and you get 6h 2m 11s.

Our original plan was to run three 2 hour sessions a day!

Post run reflections

'In many ways the running was the easy part. It probably cost less energy!'

Me!

Our objective was to have as much fun as possible, whilst raising as much money as possible, by running as far as possible, by keeping it as simple as possible. I believe we achieved that.

It's ironic that during the event I could not have felt more in touch with my body and yet in the weeks that follow it feels more and more like an out-of-body experience. It's strangely hard to grasp the reality of what we achieved. Even re-reading the blog it feels like an account of two other runners. Perhaps, given time, reality will eventually dawn. Currently my feelings are more of loss rather than achievement. For three years the Jogle has held the focus of my attention. Reading, researching, planning, discussing, organising and of course training. In many ways the running was the easy part. It probably cost less energy!

But it doesn't matter how long, hard, or well you plan, you still need a huge dollop of good fortune to succeed, and we enjoyed a skip full. The longer the event the more chances there are for something to go wrong. Many elements have to fall into place for a successful outcome. Some are under a certain amount of control and can be planned for, such as fitness, but others are not, health, the weather. Just one of these could have stopped our run in its tracks. The threatened fuel strike was totally out of our control and would certainly have made it very difficult to continue as we were totally dependent on the motorhome. Although I suspect Greg did have a plan!

We were incredibly fortunate with the weather. As mentioned earlier, anyone who expressed an opinion suggested that we run Land's End to John O'Groats because of the prevailing south westerly wind. We stuck to our plan, and for 27 out of 29 days the wind came predominantly from the North East. Pretty much unheard of at this time of year. Not only did it carry us along, it also meant that rain, sleet (and snow) were kept out of our faces.

In addition, if we had started in the south we would have suffered the floods that struck the West Country and two solid weeks of rain that affected the whole of the south, making it officially the wettest drought on record. One End to End walker we met had been forced to take his shoes off to negotiate the Bristol area, the water was so deep. We would also have caught heavier snow and rain in Scotland at the end of our journey.

The only downside to travelling North to South that I discovered was the challenge of having to read the map upside down!

The injury, although a hindrance, probably saved us from going too fast and enabled us to finish. Naturally I wouldn't choose to run in such pain, but it acted as a regulator and forced us to run within our energy level. Although, in retrospect, I think the energy to manage such an injury was quite high and quite exhausting at times, both mentally and physically.

The quite extraordinary support of friends and family and total strangers who were fired by our effort and communicated via the blog was a continual inspiration and encouragement and certainly gave us much needed energy to keep going. I wasn't expecting this at all. It completely turned around what could have felt like a relatively lonely experience, especially in Scotland when we felt so far from home for such a long time. As an aside, it was extraordinary how invisible we appeared to be on the road. In towns people looked right through us, despite our bright yellow vests emblazoned with our mission! Even shopping in Asda failed to get a reaction!

Team Greg was a huge part of our success. Quite simply, without a Greg it would have been impossible. Greg's input was sacrificial and so perfect. He drove, shopped, cooked, cleaned, mothered, advised, blogged, co-ordinated, solved problems and organised all with wisdom, and I'm glad to say typical Aussie wit and good humour. His patience and understanding were outstanding.

Before we set off I asked my wife what intrigued her most about our adventure, her reply was, as always with her, swift, simple and to the point - to know how three men would get along in a motorhome for a month! I am delighted to say that despite the stresses and strains and mounting tiredness coupled with the close proximity and lack of personal space and privacy we all managed to live together incredibly well. I'm sure there were times when we were all forced to take a deep breath but never was a cross word exchanged. Of course, JT has written his own account of the Jogle and his account of life squeezed into a sardine can on wheels for a month may be entirely different! And I fully respect that! In short, another factor contributing to our success

'It's better to look back on life and say, "I can't believe I did that." Than to look back and say, "I wish I did that"'

Nathan Riley

was that the team, though untried, gelled incredibly well. Sorry to disappoint you Sue!

Would I do it again? Probably not. It is just too much to believe the circumstances above could ever fall so beautifully into place again.

In addition to all of these I add the supreme fortune of having the most wonderful wife in the world (again JT has the opportunity to disagree, as I would with him!). She hardly flinched when I first mentioned my need to run from one end of the country to the other. She simply sat back and with love and patience, supported me all the way. She even found me a woman when I needed one! The Angel of the North. Now how many wives would do that?

With hindsight, would I change anything? Not a lot. Route-wise I believe we got it pretty perfect except the last two days spent on the A9 and part of the A82. Sharon did point us towards a cycle route that would have taken us away from the A9, but it would have added 20 miles, which for us would have been another day. As it happened the injury caused by the A9 could have cost us a good deal more than that, so who knows? Considering we did no physical recce of the route beforehand I think it was pretty much perfect and we could have expected no more.

A minor point, we took too much food with us. It was no problem to shop en route and space in the van was valuable. And that's it. The rest in my opinion was about as good as it could get.

We submitted our time to the Blackheath & Bromley Harriers AC for consideration as a club record in the hope that it might be recognised and inspire others to have a go. Even though we have a strong history of ultra distance runners, including Lew Piper (winner of the first London to Brighton Road Race), Derek Reynolds and five times Comrades winner Jackie Mekler, we have no club records beyond the marathon distance, so it will be a great honour if accepted. No reply yet...

And what about the future? I think it has probably fulfilled the need in me for the ultimate ultra adventure so I believe it's safe to say, never again. But then, as my wife points out, I did say that after my first marathon!

Reflections of the wife

When Pete first suggested that he wanted to run from John O'Groats to Land's End I knew I couldn't say no - it was clearly something he had his heart set on. He asked me two questions, "Can I do it and will you come with me?" My answers, "Yes you can and no I won't!" After years of watching him do marathons and ultra marathons (seriously, watching paint dry is more exciting!) I knew I wasn't the right person to support him in this venture. Firstly, I'd never drive a camper van off the drive let alone the length of the country! Cooking, cleaning, washing smelly kit and being a full time nurse, physio and psychologist - hmm, why don't you ask Greg! I'll be at home when you get back!

But it was OK, it was 2009 and he wasn't planning on doing it until 2012 and a lot can happen in three years! However, no sooner had I said OK, if that's what you want to do, than the house suddenly became full of maps and atlases of all kinds and every day was full of comments like "...did you know, the distance from here to here is ...", "...well, I didn't know that was there...", "...I can't believe how long the A9 is..." to which I generally replied, 'Wow, no I didn't, how interesting..." As the three years went on and people started asking me questions about it, I realised that I needed to pay more attention!

2012 dawned with great excitement, the Olympics in London, the Queen's Diamond Jubilee and Pete's big run from one end of the country to the other. Soon after Christmas the house became full of all sorts of other paraphernalia, a massage table, a microwave, more running shoes than you've ever seen in your life and the final preparation panic started. I had suggested that we organise an Ocado shopping delivery the day before they left so that they could take vital supplies with them. It was one of the funniest things ever, the Ocado man arrived, started to carry the shopping up the steps to the house and we diverted him to the motorhome, £300 of shopping was dropped off in the doorway of the van and it took two hours to find a home for it all - a significant amount of it stayed in its little home for the whole month and came back again! Apparently there are supermarkets the whole length of the British Isles!

And so they left! People had asked me what I was going to do while Pete was away, the answer was eat cheese (we don't normally - Pete doesn't like it) and do anything I wanted, so I went back to bed and had lasagne for lunch! Within an hour of them leaving Greg had posted pictures of central London on Facebook and a few hours later there were more. And that was the start of being part of the adventure electronically, which I hadn't really thought about.

I set my new ipad to the virginmoneygiving site, the tracking website and the blog site. Every time I came home I checked in to see where they were, how much money they'd raised and what they had said on the blog. After a day or two, the blog became very exciting with all sorts of people commenting on it and there was a real feel of a whole community being involved with this run not just the three people in the van. It was very exciting and it was probably at this point that I realised the enormity of what they were doing, it wasn't just madness it was actually something rather special and all was good... until day 6...

Pete had an injury in his foot and he wasn't sure he was going to be able to carry on. Hmm, this is what his mother had feared most and I knew that the rest of life would be tricky if he didn't complete what he had set out to do. For those of you who don't know Pete well, he's a perfectionist who never half does anything and the person he's hardest on is himself. By day10 the injury was so bad that he had to walk the 30 miles and they didn't finish until 9pm. It was looking grim and when Greg phoned me I knew we had a real problem.

By now they were in the Lake District so I got on my iPad and looked for sports therapists in the Cumbria area. My heart raced when I found

Everything packed - now just the food to squeeze in. Shouldn't take long!

Kathryn, a physiotherapist who specialised in End to Enders. I phoned Pete early in the morning and told him, "I've found you a woman!" They phoned her and I'm sure you've read the rest of the story already. Needless to say the medical opinion was to stop and rest the foot but I knew that would never happen! It's now almost a year since he finished the run and the foot still isn't fully recovered but regular physio and small amounts of running are moving it in the right direction - I'm still reminding him that he's lucky he can think of running a marathon again. He ran 650 miles on a damaged foot, that could have wrecked his running career forever!

Welcome party over and the van is emptied into our living room

I can't complete this part of the story without mentioning the wonderful praying ladies (and Mike) who didn't ask questions, offer medical advice or phone him and tell him to come home but prayed fervently that he would be able to complete his quest in as little pain as possible. I'm sure he has said that the man on the bike who led him to the podiatrist couldn't possibly have been a coincidence. Thank you God!

Well, I think that might be the end of my story. Once Pete had a heel lift in his shoe he was able to run again, the blog continued to fascinate and more people got involved, it stayed exciting right up until the moment that they arrived back safely - I still miss it!

Apparently, he has proved himself to the world and he doesn't need to do anything else - we'll see...

Greg and Peter return to a hero's welcome from family, neighbours and friends

(JT and Maz came back later)

Acknowledgements (Thanks!)

The danger here, of course, is that I miss someone out, but I must take that risk. And to avoid further offence... it's alphabetical!

In addition to those mentioned specifically I would also like to thank all those who sponsored us so generously and also all those who followed us on our journey and contributed to the blog.

Thank you!

Jack Adams (The Land's End John O'Groats Association) - For your invaluable information culled from Joglers and Lejogers past and present.

Alison, Jimmy, Sandy, James and his wife - For turning up and shouting GO!

Blackheath & Bromley Harriers AC - I'm not entirely sure you understood, but you generously supported us with great enthusiasm and comradeship. It's an honour to be one of you.

Rory Coleman - So glad we met you & the team on the way up. Your advice and route were invaluable. We couldn't have done it without your input.

The Cure Parkinson's Trust - Theresa, Helen ('Q'), Anna and Tom. Your work and organization are truly inspirational. This isn't the end of the road.

Greg Dwyer - The real hero of this adventure. All we had to do was eat, run and sleep. Greg did all the rest - and it would fill another book...see post run reflections. Greg - I will ALWAYS be grateful to you.

Ollie Dwyer - Huge thanks for the loan of your Dad.

Sharon Gayter - Sincere thanks for your generous support, timely encouragement and valuable advice. We were blessed to have you with us.

Ania & Ricki Gibbs (Wild Horizon) - You, and the motorhome, accommodated all our needs so perfectly.

David Greaves - Thanks for the introduction to Ram Tracking.

Gil John - Your running style was the inspiration that enabled me to carry on when it all looked so bleak. You will never know how grateful I am.

Glen Keegan - Our first sponsor and generous poster printer.

Dave & Caroline Leal - Always there. And Caroline, what a supreme effort, 30 rows of knitting a day to produce the most amazing scarf representing our journey - it should be in a gallery. Thank you.

Mike Martineau - Four you're grate proof reeding. Tank you!

Morecambe & Wise - Your 'Positive Thinking' kept us going.

Nick Nuttall - Words can't do your kindness and enthusiasm justice. Physio and all round provider extraordinaire. A privilege to have you aboard.

OffExploring.com - Great service chaps! Terrific personal responses to my requests.

Kathryn Osborne (The Angel of the North) - For me, you were the star of the show.

Mike Peel & Terri Shotton - I'm not sure how you did it, but our pictures seemed to appear on the Club Website before I'd even sent them! And the evening we spent with you was so very much appreciated.

Physios: Lauren, Sarah & Rob - For putting Humpty together again.

Questor: Sarah Niblow, for very generous extended motorhome cover.

Les Roberts - For your introduction to The Cure Parkinson's Trust and invaluable Jogle advice from your own experience.

Pauline Rogers (Mum) - For the genes, but above all the inspiration. It would/could never have happened without you.

Sue Rogers (wife) - No diamond could be big enough to express my thanks, but I'm sure you will think of something.

Henry Stalins, Natalie Easton, Jack Royle, Graham Hollingdale (Hexx) - A terrific team. Your amazing Hi-viz running vests kept us safe and helped to raise valuable sponsorship. Thank you for your enthusiasm and Hexxeptionally generous support.

Helen Stephen - Great hug!

James Taylor (RAM Tracking) - Where would we have been without you? No one would have known! Thank you for all the hard work.

Tomo - Our most enthusiastic supporter, piper and pasty provider extraordinaire. You added some much needed colour.

Woosie Turnbull - For sort of coaching me.

John E Turner - What a great adventure! You are the greatest inspiration, you taught me how to make the impossible possible. Sorry I slowed you down - but we only bloody did it!

Maz Turner - Behind every successful man is a surprised woman. Thank you for sharing your best friend with me. (And also the chocolate fingers.)

Val, Vicki, Ann, Anna, Sue, Sarah & Mike - Your reward is in heaven.

Vicki Ash - You made running a piece of cake, several times over!

John Wray (Branded Promotional Products) - Without your generous gift we would never have known where to start or finish each day. If anyone ever needs a red ball - I'll point them in your direction!

The 100 Marathon Club - Fellow members of the 'extreme end of normal' club, we thank and salute you and hold you all in the highest regard.

You *all* deserve a sticker!

LANDS END 2012
NEW YORK 3147
JOHN O'GROATS 874
ISLES OF SCILLY 28
LONGSHIPS LIGHTHOUSE 1½
SHAKE JOGLE & ROLL
21ST MAY
TEXT
LEGS70
70070

'Only those who will risk going too far can possibly find out how far they can go.'

T S Eliot

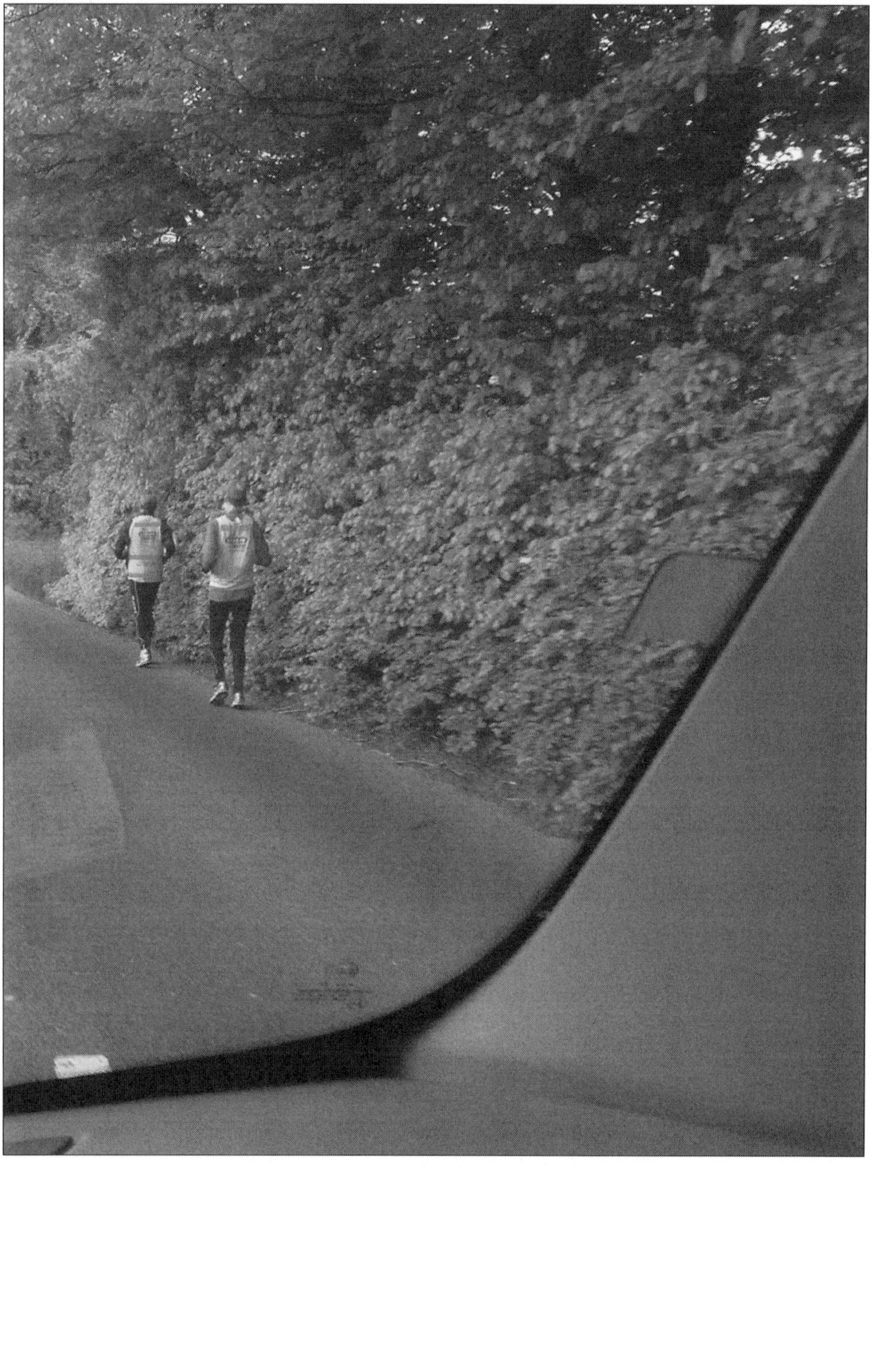

The view from the driver's seat

What makes a guy travel halfway around the world to drive a camper for two people mad enough to run 50km a day for a month?

Greg's story

Introduction

What makes a guy travel halfway around the world to drive a camper for two people mad enough to run 50km a day for a month? It's a question I was asked many times by friends and family as I accepted the request some three years ago to join – then Pete – on his own as he headed on his journey from John O'Groats to Lands End. But firstly, how does a guy from Australia get involved in such an ambitious journey?

I first met Pete through Sue back in '98. Sue was a work colleague I became friends with as I worked at St. John's and St. Clement's as part of the normal Australian thing of exploring Europe by working as a teacher in London. One thing led to another and Sue indicated that her husband 'ran', and so like many long lasting friendships my relationship with Pete and Sue began through the mutual like and affinity with a sporting pursuit. Our first run around Dulwich Park, led to other runs and many hours of running throughout the Greater London area.

In my time working with Sue, Pete and I ran several races together, half marathons – and the shock of all horrors a proper 10km race at Marwell Zoo, the setting for the movie Fierce Creatures. I say a proper 10km race as every other event was conducted in imperial measurements, something I refused to get into and discuss even when talking about the Jogle.

Pete and I would be discussing the Jogle over Skype – our constant communication tool, often during my working hours as a classroom teacher. In fact there were many a time that Pete and I would have a conversation while he and Sue were sitting in bed and I'd introduce both of them to a throng of happy Australian children. The conversation would go like this:

Pete: *(Posh English accent – according to the children in my classes.)* So I'll be travelling slightly more than 30 miles a day.

Greg: Crikey mate – you mean 50km.

Pete: My dear fellow – 30 miles.

Greg: Yes Pete – 50 km.

Child: What's a mile?

As the date got closer and the details of the adventure became apparent – there were to be two runners, Pete and John – a crusty 60 year old beer drinking connoisseur. I first met John as Pete and I were heading out on a 32 km run throughout London – again in 1998.

So the Jogle adventure and organization was complete; and the date was set for April-May 2012. My preparation was easy – I learnt to drive a 6m vehicle – drink beer, and read a map (iphone). I didn't worry about learning how to convert mileage, 50km a day is simple – it's a nice round number.

I arrived in London refreshed from the 26 hour journey and headed to pick up the camper, and continue my training by sampling the beer drinking with Pete's sons, who I could no longer throw around willy nilly.

Saying goodbye to Pete and Sue's youngest son Maff back in 1998. I must have made a good impression or our friendship would never have lasted so long!

The journey begins

My other view of the Jogle

After all the final preparations John, Pete and I left in the camper – and headed through central London on our journey.

Unlike Pete and John I didn't keep a diary, I like to take photos – I'm Australian, ritin' is 'ard work – just ask Pete how long he's waited for this transcript.

Following are 30 observations on the adventure – centred around all that I witnessed and learnt– yes it's in point form, and in a random order, everything I now record is true – honest!

1. A six sleeper motorhome, for 3 blokes travelling together for a month is just big enough. But if you're going to do something similar – get a bus or at least one with 'captain chairs'.

2. My preparation of learning to control a six metre vehicle was very valuable – Pete's preparation didn't include this training – just ask the Land Rover and Motorbike.

3. Even though one may run for 6 hours a day for a month doesn't mean that you need to shower every day – though changing your socks and shoes every two hours is most important.

Forget the motorhome - next time we hire one of these!

4   You can live in a camper for a month and not wash your bed sheets once!

5   Hard boiled eggs are not that difficult to cook – even though none were cooked.

6   Having a camper plastered with signage about a charity run – doesn't mean that everyone will read what the signage says – and will still ask what's going on.

7   The generosity of people – very random and kind people – continued to astound me. Like the guy who paid 50 quid towards the fuel I was getting at a servo near Bristol.

8   The police don't like it when you park a 6m vehicle directly under the flight path of inbound jet aircraft.

9   The border crossing between Scotland and England is naff! Considering it's just about halfway! Better signage would be greatly appreciated.

10 Chicken Parmas are very easy to cook – and will satisfy two hungry runners with an appetite.

11 Stopping in a pub to read a book while waiting for Pete and John isn't always a good idea as you may not be able to drive for a while.

12 Tomo is a legend and a top bloke. Enough said!

13 When going to the toilet outside the camper, check you can't be spotted in the side mirrors.

14 The plethora of beers available throughout the UK is startling. John gave me the challenge that each day we had to have a new beer from the local region. I readily accepted.

15 It doesn't matter how late you're home from the pub – two guys running 50km a day won't hear you no matter how much noise you make.

16 To scare yourself sh**less go stay in a small out of the way, back country camping spot, and while there watch League of Gentleman.

Head of advertising, just one of my many jobs

Seriously - is this the best you can do?

Pete enjoying some privacy

Above: Another long wait for the lads

Right: Beautiful cycling country (at the foot of Glen Coe)

17   Ipads are awesome – Pete and John were generous enough to provide me with an ipad so that I could take photos – update the blog, and keep in contact with home.

18   Paying 50 quid so that your husband loses his beard and moustache as a hidden bet is a bloody good idea.

19   Scotland is a wonderful, beautiful place. Even John O'Groats has it's lovely side.

20   Big caravan parks aren't always the best caravan parks – small caravan parks can be very scary.

21   Avoid caravan parks that have a token for the use of washing machines or driers, they are often very expensive.

22   Learning how to put up a yurt tent was fantastic and not really part of the planned adventure.

23   The people we met also doing the Jogle each had their own story – own unique style – mostly their own charity – and the beauty was there wasn't any competition about who was more or less noble. It was wonderful.

24. Not everything that you buy on a Jogle journey can go into the 'Pool Room'.

25. Cornish Pasties should only be bought from Cornwall.

26. Pete doesn't drink red wine all that often – the morning after can be quite funny.

27. Wild camping makes it a true sense of adventure.

28. I would hate to play John in a game of scrabble – however, I'd love him to be on my team at a trivia night – his knowledge is often better than 'Google'. I started to refer to him as 'Joogle'.

29. Thank you to all those who gave generously throughout the run. Made all of the many hours of lazing around reading books, driving however I liked ('cause I had a six metre vehicle), watching movies, drinking beer worthwhile.

30. Pete and John are two very amazing, talented, headstrong individuals who have the ability to push themselves through pain and suffering without complaining. They are to be congratulated for their amazing achievement.

Top: The morning after!

Below: Just time to buy a few souvenirs before catching up with the lads

So, what makes a guy travel halfway around the world to drive a camper for two people mad enough to run 50km a day for a month? In essence the answer is easy :- Friendship, a sense of adventure, watching the UK go past at approximately 3.2km/h, the opportunity to help someone reach a life-long ambition while raising money for a good cause.

Enough said!

I would like to dedicate this memoir to my parents: Ernest Harry Turner (1912-2005) and Pauline Mary Turner (1911-2009). The tribute to my Mum and Dad is because they never stopped travelling and asking questions. However, I would like to dedicate the run as a whole to 'Little Mazzi,' my wife of over 40 years, for allowing me to attempt the Jogle. Yes, obviously, we married while very young. We have faltered and we have struggled but we are still in there fighting. Now you can all see the problem. I would like to give her this love poem if I haven't before. Memory is not my strong suit when it comes to personal things.

What Do I Like? (About You)

What do I like?
Seagulls gliding over cliffs.
The talking of small streams.
Clouds banked over the sea.
Pounding waves on a pebbly beach.
The robin's song on a crisp, cold morning.
Smoke drifting lazily on a still summer's day.
Mirror-like reflections.
Patchwork fields seen from the top of a hill.
Stately silver birches and mighty oaks.
The smell from the sun
burning down on a herb garden.
I feel the essence of these things within you.

Trolling Down Hill

Ramblings from a tightrope with no safety net but death... or... Now that I have your complete attention

John's story

Who am I?

'Other things may change us, but we start and end with family.'

Anthony Brandt

Because this journey will no doubt be life changing, I had better note down some things that occurred when I was me. As you will notice soon, if you haven't already, I have a butterfly mind that doesn't settle for very long. The stream of consciousness is my kind of river. Being Gemini, I also have the traits of restlessness and inquisitiveness. The word on the street was/is "The Turners are mad" and full of nervous energy. I do feel that I live in a busy constant present with a few things booked in the future. However the past is mainly a mystery – how I got to be here. I do suffer from psoriasis, depression (like all other deluded great comedians), SAD (Seasonal Affective Disorder), OCD (Obsessive Compulsive Disorder) and the ability to run long distances. Though not always in that order. Having said this, I am a fairly regular guy otherwise. I know I am a superb human specimen but I have to try and live with that knowledge. Some have even compared me to Dean Karnazes (If you don't know who he is – use the internet – I have to). What I think they mean, is I resemble the thickness of one of his arms or legs.

Talking of tributes, reminds me, that I have never had a best friend. Although I have got a wife at the moment, does that count?! Just joking of course. Keep on running and don't look back. Actually, I have got a best friend at the moment. Mobile phones as we know them now, really started about 1987 or 25 years ago. In 2006/7 there were 2.5 to 3 billion subscribers or 45% of the world's inhabitants, but not me. All the way to the start of 2012 – no, not me. But then the John O'Groats to Land's End Run starts to look like a chunk of reality out there in the void and so I must have/need a mobile phone of my own I am told. So on the 6th February 2012 I get one and text Peter Rogers first. Done deal. I now have a best friend! Actually it is a very good relationship between Peter and myself. He does as he's told. We don't know a lot of things about each other, but we do know we can always ask. What I am trying to say is – we are ideally suited to our task. Bless him.

The problem is we need someone to do all the work apart from the running. Things like the cooking, washing, shopping and driving. This is why there has to be a third person in the team and I don't know Greg at all. What I shall have to use is the model of behaviour from my mother's family. She had a brother two years older than her and a sister two years older than that. If there was any trouble and it didn't matter who was the main culprit/instigator, the youngest (my mother) was sent to her room, which almost certainly in those days was their room as well. No bedroom each in those days. Maz shared a bedroom in Battersea with her brother until she was thirteen years old and he was ten and their parents lived in Wandsworth. No, only joking. So, sorry Greg, but any trouble, its nighty night. Anyway, my Mum used to love it. She got into bed in the peace and quiet and read or day-dreamed while looking out of the window, if they had one of course. Things were a bit thin in those days between the Great Wars.

Friends know that I do like a pint or two of the singing syrup as my old boss used to call it. A pint of real ale is a joy to hold. I have a lot of beer in my family history. My mother was born in a public house in Bath. Also, my maternal grandfather was a brewer's clerk and the paternal grandfather a brewer's drayman. My father and his sister both worked for the Courage Brewery.

I don't remember much about my youth but I do know I ran everywhere and still do. In Britain there are 38 million drivers, but not me. Going back to our family again, I find it unbelievable that just my father's father – Ernest Frederick, was born on 11th June 1866 and here am I in 2012. Unfortunately, I never knew him but if you look at his photo, he sure had a mean pair of long running legs on him. What stands out in my mind was being cold although I am pretty hardy now. I was the

L-R. My Granddad, Ernest Frederick Turner, born 1866. My Father, who did a 5 mile charity walk in the City of London when he was over 90 years old. And me, playing for 'Hairy Fairies United'

109

Me before I grew the beard

Anyone for tennis? My mother in 1937

concentration camp kid. There I was standing on an English south coast beach and this is in the height of summer – August most probably – blue skin shuddering and teeth chattering wildly. I was quite unable to dress myself and certainly could not do up buttons. I can feel every bit of this as I write. It is as fresh as yesterday. You could see all my ribs and play them like a xylophone. I am not much different in the physique stakes currently. One thing has changed. My legs are now strong but my arms are still weak. I can just run with a water bottle, if I have to.

Thunder and lightning is another good subject to get me going on. I do not like it at all. This is how it has run through my family for the last five generations. My grandmother in Bath was an expert. It is a shame we do not know her pre-history on this subject. Her way of dealing with a storm was to take all her hairpins out, hide cutlery away, turn the mirrors round to face the wall and to open the front and back doors wide so if there was a fireball/thunderbolt it could come in the hall, track around the furniture a bit, then to disappear into their backyard. What chance did we have. My dear mother got it in a milder form. She would panic on a Monday if she heard on the weather forecast that there would be thunder and lightning on Thursday. As the day neared she would feel physically sick and then if it happened she would either hide in the cupboard under the stairs, in our baronial hallway, with the Hoover and Dad's very rarely used golf clubs, some bottles of wine and port, which she would tip upside down to clean! A set of carpet bowls and a sad variety of umbrellas and walking sticks. This wasn't such a great place to hide after my father had the cupboard changed into the downstairs toilet. The other option was to lie in the lounge on the sofa with a large cushion over her head until the Gods had finished moving their furniture about up in the sky or she had suffocated.

Now we come to me. As a third generation sufferer I was not so maladjusted as my mother. To this day I do not like severe weather in any form. I feel nervous and wish it was all over. My Mum and Dad used to have a caravan perched on the cliff top at Walmer, near Dover. There were often storms out in the English Channel and I could watch these fantastic light shows without any fear but if it came inland and the earth shook, that would leave me like a jelly. Maz does not mind

Happy days! My sister Janet and me, excited by Dad's train set

them at all. When our two daughters, Claire and Zoë, were junior school age, we would take them to the window, especially at night, to watch Mother Nature unleash her power. I would stand slightly behind them digging my long finger nails into my palms. This strategy worked and they have grown up to be fairly normal, well as far as storms are concerned. We were looking after our eldest grandson, George, one day and suddenly the heavens opened and the sky began to flash and boom. He went to the patio doors and just said while pointing "Dunderdorms". Since that day I have never been quite as scared because I just hear that word and think of a Harry Potter character. So we have managed over the course of one century to change our feelings about natural phenomena.

Another strange thing about our family is that I have a sister, Janet, who is three years older than me. If she had been born a decade prior to me I could understand it, but the weird thing is – I should have known her – but I didn't. One of the only things I can remember was being told where to stand with her in one of Dad's unnaturally posed holiday snapshots. We both hated doing this and we would muck about in a very 1950's way by being awkward and surly. The pictures we still have are real set pieces with child dummies in a landscape. Of course, I know now the difficulty of trying to get a decent photograph of your offspring for posterity. It is not so traumatic these days because you can just press delete and have another go but back then every single one of these sad black and white images was going to cost hard earned money. Nothing to laugh about then. After our parents got older and then passed away we have come to enjoy having a sibling and we love each other which is a very nice feeling. But where were you Janet? In the cupboard under the stairs until a storm came and mum needed it!

There are a lot of other things I just don't understand. The Internet is one of them. I don't know what I was doing particularly but I turned my back for a second, took my eye off of the ball and when I re-engaged with the world, everything that has ever been, was searchable via a computer. Now who did that and when? I am talking about a trillion things and they just got logged up seemingly overnight. I was a librarian for twenty six years and I know how hard it can be to reference answers for people. I blinked and it has all been made traceable. The other thing that gets me is 'predictive texting'. If it has not been done already I would like to write the first novel completely in that medium. It is amazing what comes up in this format: KISS is LIPS and DAUGHTER is FATIGUES.

Because I don't cook I do a lot of washing up and I really enjoy it, if there aren't too many saucepans. Nine out of ten of my bright ideas come while swishing about the dirty cups and plates. Do you ever get the thought come into your head that civilization (although not very civil is it?) is at about twenty seconds to midnight in the scheme of things. Total destruction is just around the corner. Then I think please can I be the last one left to switch off the lights and close the door. At least I would know then how the whole plot finally played out. I get this come through to me every couple of days. Hey! Someone seriously

Winner of 'Best Beard' in the London Marathon?

screwed up my head years ago. And then I think "No" we'll survive. The world has continued after the fall of the other civilizations whether Aztec, Greek or Roman. But this is the first one where, because of computers, mobile phones and satellites – we are the same civilization whether we are in Britain, New Zealand or Mongolia. The disease of 'modern living' has infected the whole planet at the same time. So it will all go down together. I used to watch people scribbling page after page of large writing when I was working in the reference library and now I do it myself. Unfortunately I don't make this stuff up.

My Mum and Dad were married for just over sixty five years and they courted for seven. However, my Dad always said that if he had not married he would have liked to be a monk. I always wanted to be a really cool Buddhist but I had the wrong O' levels and not enough. I think inside I am a nice hippie, but with layers of other stuff, not all good, on top. Our careers advisor at school had other ideas. It was obvious to him I was best suited for a job in Customs & Excise, which actually, I think I might have liked. When I left school my mother set about finding me a position. I rather liked the one sitting down with my feet up. She saw in the local paper that the council had vacancies in some of its departments. She asked me what would be my favourites out of about ten different ones. I chose Public Health, Housing and Libraries from the list. The letter was duly sent off and a reply came back that there were only places left in the libraries. I had to go to the main library where I spoke to the man doing the interviews, for about twenty minutes, all about athletics and running history. He said I should start the following week. So I then did twenty six years in the library service.

Fancy dress was never a problem for me!

Working in the library really did appeal to me. I did and do like books and people. It was nicer than a book shop because there was not the financial side to deal with, apart from the occasional overdue charges. It was my university because I would get asked hundreds of questions a day and if I did not know the answer at least I had the relevant tools to find it. We worked hard and did long hours for not a large salary. The advantage was in the holiday entitlement and the varied hours. When I started in 1968 the branch stayed open until 8pm on four weekdays and each member of staff had to work two of these. It was a nine o'clock start going through to the evening with an hour for lunch and half an

Don't let this man in or out of the country. Recognise the hat?

Barcelona Olympics 1992. (Ready but not needed)

hour off before you started the last session. You also had to work on two Saturdays to get one off. But I only needed to do four hours on a Monday and I had the whole of Thursday off. I always tried to get into the reference library on a late night, as although it was well used, most people just got on with their task and I could get stuck into learning the Oxford English Dictionary from the letter 'Z' backwards. This came in very useful many years later when I was working for Croydon Council in the Asylum Seekers Team. The office was pretty manic for much of the working week so we always tried on a Friday afternoon to wind things down and get off early to the pub. We even used to try and find time for a little general (only if you knew the answers) knowledge quiz. We had a very diverse collection of staff and some very keen brains. One particular afternoon I had been performing rather well and another colleague thought, in a nice way, that I should be thwarted. What a wonderful word that is. It sounds like a medieval torture where your spleen is extracted out through your nose. Anyway, I digress. I saw this workmate was on the phone but I did not realize what he was getting up to. He had rung through to our other office and asked them to select a question to stump me with. Unfortunately, Richard just grabbed his dictionary off the shelf and turned to the last pages. Justin put his phone down, leant back in his swivel chair, put his hands behind his head and with a definite smirk (which I think should be a freshwater fish) on his face, uttered the fatal words "Where do you stand on ZWINGLI?" I looked out of the window for a moment, almost as if I had not heard the question and then turned to him with a puzzled frown on my face. I leant back in my swivel chair, put my hands behind my head and said very slowly, "If you mean, Ulrich Zwingli, 1484-1531, the Swiss leader of the Reformation, do you know, I'm not sure." His mouth opened wide but nothing came out of it. He got up and ran the whole length of a long office jumping up and down with merry rage. It was an exceedingly funny moment and I am just glad that I was there to witness it. It was an office that did have a lot of laughs but this could not have been set up any better. We then went down the pub and I took up my usual role of making sure afterwards that all the well-oiled personnel made it to the right houses with the right people. What a spoilsport. Every week got to be mayhem, just like a works' Christmas do. There would be people taking photos of bits of their anatomy in the loo, others falling over tables full of bottles and much leaving of wallets and clothing when we left for the next hostelry. I think one of the ladies lost a different coat in a different pub four weeks in a row and had to ring around from the office on a Monday morning, trying to locate them. The likes of that office will never be seen again. Shame. All thanks must go to Richard B.

As you will see when you look at the daily entries for our trip, I have always liked funny sounding words and place names.

TROLLING DOWN HILL
(GREEN STREET GREEN ROAD)

Foreword No.1

Hi. Apparently I am about to embark on a one month long running adventure for a charity: the Cure Parkinson's Trust. It was in 1817 that London doctor, James Parkinson (1755-1824) published 'An essay on the shaking palsy' and established Parkinson's disease as a recognized medical condition. I do feel very privileged to be doing this at age sixty plus. When I was growing up in the 1950's, people were lucky to be alive at sixty, let alone fit and well enough to take on a challenge like John O'Groats to Land's End. It will give me a chance to see Scotland, which I have only visited for a two week holiday in Pitlochry, many years ago. Scotland is vast. I thought from a deep southerner's perspective that it was about 200 miles long. But we do not cross the border until the middle of our day thirteen out of twenty nine. We run about 375 miles before we get into England. Our run will be in total nearly 860 miles and although it starts with just one step – we might need over 623,000 steps each to finish it. When you are sitting comfortably then I'll begin. I used to be a stand up comedian but my legs can't take it these days.

I feel I ought to write a few words about Peter and Greg, but I don't know how nice to be, as I don't know what or if they have written about me. Peter thought about his project from all sides and did an unbelievable amount of planning. When you start to think about the logistics of a month away from home, it is not long before your lists become endless. We did not have that many meetings together, although we could discuss items whilst on long training runs. For a few weeks he must have thought he was married to a map. We were under pressure because no matter how you arranged things to cover all eventualities it was still always going to be a physical event. We trained, we got well underway and then an injury springs up out of the blue yonder. I hope Peter has written about the mental and physical pain he went through to achieve his dream.

I must now try to quantify the input of one Greg Dwyer. To say, that it would have been mission impossible without him, is the only true place to start. I also feel that there is a Mount Everest angle to this story. Peter and I, were the Sir Edmund Hillary part and Greg played the Nepalese Sherpa, Tenzing Norgay. Some people can be easily forgotten – what was his name again? Ah yes – Greg. I liked him very much, as he was a practical and physical character, but in a totally different way from me. He knew an army marches on its stomach as well as the legs. As soon as we had finished our daily mileage, the food began to appear. We would climb into the van to be assaulted by the wonderful smell of soup with either garlic bread or chips. This was one of the best parts of each day. We would arrive at the campsite and be sent off to shower and change, as quickly as was possible, in our sometimes sorry state. When we helped each other back up the steps into the van, there on the table would be a marvellous meal of meat, vegetables and pasta with a sauce. After all the sandwiches and crisps it was heavenly.

Apart from looking after us, he had a long list of chores to accomplish, just like a real wife! He had to buy all the shopping and petrol, do all the washing and drying, cooking and driving, take photos and deal with the campsites. We also hoped he could enjoy a cycling holiday, but never mind, eh!

Another Poem

Dare not die yet - not today, anyway

I have far flung friends to greet again
Enemies to forgive.
Lies to undo and hurts to heal.
I am nowhere near ready yet.
I want to go out in one flash of pure light.
I want to laugh a lot more.
And there's more crying to be done.
Ideas to be born, promises to fulfil.
I want to tie the laces of my life
Into a perfect bow.
I don't want to 'come as you are'
I want to go when I'm set.

Foreword No. 2

Next time we will fly up to John O'Groats. No, not really, because there won't be a next time. It was quite harrowing taking a two day drive to get to your start point and seeing that 80% of it was downhill, thereby uphill, for us on the run.

Bleak is a very kind word for John O'Groats. Think more the derelict remains of the place that time forgot, and then on a bad day. You really are at the end or beginning of something. The weather was actually what they most probably describe as 'kind'. There was a bracing breeze but it was clear of rain so that we could see the islands offshore. I had to go to the facilities at about 4am. It was cold and windy but the stars were incredible. With so little light pollution nearby you felt you could have pulled them out of the sky just by reaching up.

JOHN
O'GROATS
2012
LANDS END 874
PENTLAND SKERRIES 6
SHAKE JOGLE & ROLL
23RD APRIL
ORKNEY &
SHETLAND ISLES
TEXT
0

Monday 23 April - St George's Day - John O'Groats - Lybster | **Day 1**

Working nine to five

30 miles

Our daily running schedule was to be from 9am to 5pm. The alarm was to go off at 7am and we would do everything necessary to be at our start point for 9am. Then we would run from 9am to 11am, eat and drink and rest until 12.00. Then run until 2pm and eat and drink and rest until 3pm. Then run to whenever we reached the thirty mile point which we hoped would be by 5pm. Of course this changed pretty quickly after Peter damaged his foot and we needed to run shorter segments with more icing to the affected area. The rest of the day never seemed to follow our cunning plan. We estimated that between 5pm and 6pm we would have a bite to eat, change into comfortable and dry clothes and then go to the campsite for that night. From 6pm until lights out at 10pm it would be a matter of setting up camp, putting the washing on, showering ourselves, eat dinner, massage, debrief and take our underpants off, kill the comedian, plan next day, write up the log and diary, then go to sleep. The reality included standing in a loch, going to the pub, driving around to try and find somewhere to get a signal for our various devices, entertaining a mixed bag of strangers and friends, licking our wounds, playing electronic Scrabble with three or four people in the world simultaneously, texting family, drinking some of the day's catch of beer, looking at maps, wondering what you do with three socks - no don't answer this, trying to hide chocolate finger biscuits and finally turning out the light about midnight!

It's traditional for End to Enders to dip their feet in the sea at the start and finish of the challenge...the rocks were very slippery so we used a rock pool!

Great placename of the day:
SHELLOW BOWELLS
(Essex)
It sounds like I felt the night before starting.

Running in honour of:
'ALF' AFRED SHRUBB
1879-1964
Passed away on St George's Day. He won over 1,000 races - amateur & professional. He was so good he ran against relay teams. In a one hour race in 1904 he ran 11 miles 1137 yards. This was not broken until 1951. 28 world records.
Also for Number One
PAULINE ROGERS
Peter's mum - without whom...

Word of the day:
SKEDADDLE
To run off hastily.

Quote for the day:
'Planning engages the mind and gives expression to your motivation.'
Mike Cudahy

121

Day 2

60 miles

Tuesday 24 April - Lybster - Brora

100 green bottles...

Great placename of the day:
STANFORD DINGLEY *(Berkshire)*
I had one of these but the handle fell off.

Running in honour of:
SYDNEY CHARLES WOODERSON MBE 1914-2006
Blackheath Harrier. 'The Mighty Atom'. World record for one mile: 4min 06.4 in 1937. He was very versatile as he won the National Cross Country in 1948.

Word of the day:
WHIRLIGIG
Spinning toy. Merry-go round.

Quote for the day:
'The measure of who we are is what we do with what we have.'
Vince Lombardi

This day started something we had never envisaged. I like my beer and so does Greg. I set him a task for the trip, to try and get a bottle of local beer every day, as we came down the map. I thought he would buy one and at about 9pm we would share it, discuss its merits or faults, then night night lights out. This is the way it started but then Greg got into his Tasmanian stride and was going to supermarkets, village corner shops and off licences. I think one day he produced six different ones at our evening meal! Just to make sure our driver didn't over imbibe I had to suffer two or maybe three myself. Sweet dreams baby.

The other part of this alcoholic story was not intentional. Because we needed wi-fi in the evenings, so that we could put out our jewels of journalism to the waiting world, however tired, we had to go into pubs. We arrived at the Sutherland Inn at Brora both a bit blitzed by the second thirty miler in a row and having expected to be cosily tucked away in our bunk beds by this hour. Stepping down out of the mother ship onto the gravel covered carpark, I thought to myself, my feet must be really tender, but upon looking down the cause was obvious. Both Peter and I were wearing our slippers and I am surprised we were not wearing pyjamas. One thing that taking on a large venture does is to loosen your inhibitions. We thought they most probably would not look at our feet and if they did - who cares? Men on a mission and all that.

All I can remember about this hostelry was that it had on sale over 500 whiskies and one beer that was not very good. Whether my memory is correct, but I think they had a large book you could order the whisky from and that some reached £50 for a nip. After this adventure we went into other pubs and even hotels clad in our slippers. One was the Avon Gorge Hotel, a very swanky place in Clifton, where we trundled in to use our physio Nick's bath (me) and massage table (Peter).

The big countdown of miles takes on its optimistic face. Tomorrow we have less than 800 miles to go.

Wednesday 25 April - Brora - Golspie | **Day 3**

The A9 forever. Hope not.

90 miles

Great place names here in Scotland. They should be recited slowly in a rich deep voice. The Falls of Shin. The Sands of Nigg (this one sounds like it is straight out of Monty Python). The Hill of Many Stanes and the Storehouse of Foulis. I think I hear bagpipes, but we have to wait almost a month more for that pleasure. Yes, I do really like them!

The wind was very strong as we ran over the bridge that spans the Dornoch Firth. The only other time I have had my face forced sideways was at the top of Ditchling Beacon during the London to Brighton race one year. Luckily, however hard it blew this time, there was no rain with it.

Great placename of the day:
HOPTON WAFERS
(Shropshire)
Very nice with a cup of coffee.

Running in honour of:
JACKIE MEKLER
Blackheath Harrier. Won the Comrades Marathon in South Africa 5 times. Was also second twice and third twice. In 1960 he was the first to break 6 hours (5.56.32) for this double marathon.

Word of the day:
CONUNDRUM
A riddle.

Quote for the day:
I made this up all on my own.
A Scottish Haiku Like Thing. 2012.
'Keiss, Reiss.
Papigoe, Staxigoe.
Occumster, Thrumster.'
All real place names in the area.

123

Day 4 — **Thursday 26 April - Golspie - Beauly**

120 miles

The charge of the light brigade

Great placename of the day:
MELBURY BUBB
(Dorset)
Don't put too many gooseberries in or you can ruin the recipe.

Running in honour of:
GEOFFREY NICHOLLS
1928-2008
Personal friend

Word of the day:
WOBBLE
Vibrate unsteadily.

Quote for the day:
'Two it takes to start a quarrel, one can always end it.'
Anon

A fortunate day - in the end. The wind was still coming from behind us and only a little light rain. We also finished our dicing with death on the A9. We ended up recording a good marathon time and 30 mile time although these figures are just for interest as it is the fact that we finish and feel good that matters. We have always trained light, to avoid injury and fatigue and yet again the theory appears to be working.

Clockwise: Peter out in the cold waiting for a satellite signal

The Jogle Brothers on the road

'We were on a break!'

124

Friday 27 April - Beauly - Fort Augustus Day 5

Clear behind. That's nice to know. 150 miles

This was the morning when I had my first major panic. The first section of the day involved a switchback of ups and downs. This was quite difficult enough, then a drop of blood fell out of my nose. Am I imagining things. Let's have a spit. A red glob appears on the black tarmac. Never experienced this before. Are we already overdoing things? Do I tell Peter? On we run with me trying not to breathe, swallow or spit. This is useless. Spit again - blood again. So I say to Peter, "Lovely here, don't worry, I'm spitting up blood, thought it best to tell you." I cannot remember his answer. The hills were so steeply down at this point that we were walking with thigh agony and by the time we reached the van the drama had ceased. Where this problem came from and where it went I have no idea. Just very grateful I had no other problem of this nature.

Great placename of the day:
UFTON NERVET
(Berkshire)
Sorry about the smell.

Running in honour of:
MICHAEL 'BRUCE' SWINTON TULLOH
Born: 29.9.1935
In 1969 he ran 2876 miles across America from Los Angeles to New York in 64 days. Also won European 5000m championship in 1958.

Word of the day:
LOZENGE
Diamond shaped.

Quote for the day:
'Pain is only temporary - pride is forever.'
Don Diablo

125

Day 6   **Saturday 28 April - Fort Augustus - Fort William**

180 miles   Steak out

Great placename of the day:

FARLEIGH WALLOP
(Hampshire)
What a nice pint of beer.

Running in honour of:

CAVIN WOODWARD
1947-2010

Won London to Brighton race in 1975. Also in 1975 he set 100 mile track world best of 11 hours 38 minutes 54 seconds. In the same race he set 50 mile, 100k and 150k records. He said "My distaste for training is aggravated when I find I have to train by myself." He loved to race. Same for me.

Word of the day:

BIZARRE
Strange in appearance.

Quote for the day:

'You can only be young once, but you can be immature for ever.'
Paul Gambaccini

A truly beautiful day. Loch Lochy (so nice they named it twice) was stunning and definitely a place I would like to return to. The Commando Memorial is in a very dramatic setting which I would advise people to visit if they get the chance.

We were in Fort William in the evening and were 180 miles in 6 days HUNGRY. There was an up-market fish restaurant on the water's edge but we found out it did also serve meat. While Greg went off to park the van, Peter and I settled into a nice table and got some drinks. Greg arrived and the waitress came to take our order. Now, I am not a great fish eater and had set my heart on a steak with a capital S. Peter didn't want to risk anything fishy in case it upset his system. Greg, I think, would have eaten anything. We ordered the steak and chips, but the waitress came back to say that it had run out. We said, "well you should have killed it. That would have stopped it in its tracks!" We were sorely disappointed, but then saw that there was another meat option. I think we would still have had it, even if it was skunk kebabs. But it was mouth watering lamb and mash potato. Ten minutes later, drinks almost finished, we were informed that even the sheep had jumped ship. This was really bad news to two people who had to run so far in a week and their roadie who had to keep them out of prison to finish the mission. When we told the lady that we would like the bill for the

The Commando Memorial, near Spean Bridge, with great views of Ben Nevis and Aonach Mòr

Note the trendy footwear   *Peter and Greg updating the world on our progress*

drinks as soon as possible as WE STILL NEEDED TO DEVOUR MOUNTAINS OF MEAT and it was getting past our bedtime, all she kept on about was how upsetting it was for her and how it had quite ruined her evening!

Greg guided us out and down the road to a large hotel. The first bad news was it had a long flight of stone stairs up to the front door. We were hungry, in our slippers and walking on feet that felt like burning coals. Inside it was all antique (it had been there a long time) carpet and very large armchairs. Yes, a bit like a nursing home on hard times. All the staff were nice except their commandant (called Hatchet Face). She paced up and down the bar breathing fire at all and sundry. (Although it was a Saturday. Get it? You will!). The other side of the coin about this place was that it served very good food. I think we ordered triple humungous burgers and sacks of fat covered potatoes. We sat there all cosy watching an amazing sunset out of an enormous bay window. I also kept trying to think of an incredibly funny one liner to get the old goat in charge to smile, for it was Saturday night. I ordered another drink and I think it was £3.10. She asked if I'd got the 10p? I said no, I was sorry I had not. She then gave me a look that turned me into a pile of salts on that carpet, tutted and said, "I shall have to put it in myself." I smiled.

127

Day 7 | Sunday 29 April - Fort William - Altnafeadh

210 miles The dream team

Great placename of the day:

KIRKBY OVERBLOW
(North Yorkshire)
A fifth sandwich is never a good idea.

Running in honour of:

TERRANCE STANLEY 'TERRY' FOX C.C.
1958-1981
Canadian humanitarian, athlete and cancer treatment activist. After losing his right leg to cancer, aged 20, he decided to run coast to coast across Canada in 1980, to raise money for research. He ran an average of a marathon a day. The cancer spread to his lung and he was forced to stop after 143 days. He had run 3339 miles. His charity has raised hundreds of millions of dollars. Now feel humble.

Word of the day:

TOGGLE
A device for fastening.

Quote for the day:

'Champions have to have the skill and the will. But the will must be stronger than the skill.'

Muhammad Ali

What a beautiful day. We ran most of the way up the Glencoe Pass and the views were spectacular. The pain at back of left knee, noticed on day two, no worse for another 150 miles on top. Tender right hamstring came into the equation today. I am eating and drinking more each day and feeling much better as a result. The weight - about half a stone - that I lost in the first couple of days has not increased.

Top: Where's Wally - and friend?

Right: The road, the weather and the mountains were so inspiring. I think today will live in our memories forever

128

Monday 30 April - Altnafeadh - Inverarnan

Day 8

In tandem

240 miles

What a difference a day makes. We step out into a blizzard. I remember Peter singing very loudly into the nothingness. We arrive back in Ardlui. This was our stop-over on the drive up from London. A beautiful place to stay. We went to the hotel bar in our slippers.

Bracing ourselves for the blizzard

Up close and personal with a local

Déjà vu... back in Ardlui - on the shores of Loch Lomond. Note the snow on the high ground

Great placename of the day:

HELIONS BUMPSTEAD
(Essex)
If you put a needle in & draw off the fluid...

Running in honour of:

EMIL ZÁTOPEK
1922-2000

Czech long distance runner. In 1952 Olympics he won gold at 5000m, 10,000m and the marathon, his first, in 2.23.03. He set 18 world records. He was known as 'the locomotive' because of his distinctive running style. His wife Dana Zátopková won gold in the javelin at the same Olympics. Like Maz and I, they were born the same day, month and year, September 19th 1922. There were only 6 hours between their births.

Word of the day:

DUNGAREE
Trousers with a bib.

Quote for the day:

'Start slow, then taper off.'
Walt Stack

129

Day 9 — **Tuesday 1 May - Inverarnan - Dumbarton**

270 miles Catharsis or bust*

Great placename of the day:
HASELBURY PLUCKNETT
(Somerset)
The chocolate with the soft centre.

Running in honour of:
BRUCE FORDYCE
Born: 1955
Won the Comrades Marathon in South Africa nine times. Eight in a row. He also won the London to Brighton race three times in a row.

Word of the day:
HARRUMPH
To make the noise of clearing the throat.

Quote for the day:
'When you're going through hell, keep going.'
Winston Churchill

But don't try looking for these places on a map

On this day, Peter's left foot became the fourth occupant of our van. Could we stop it from overwhelming us? The pain that had been caused by jumping up and down verges on the A9 for the first few days, reared its ugly foot again. The verges were very soft from all the rain and the roads were very hard old tarmac. So the constant changes had set up a bad reaction between skin and bone. Greg advised Peter to put his foot in some cold water to help the swelling and pain. I thought this would call for a bucket, but when I came down from my top bunk, Peter was standing way out in Loch Lomond up to a considerable depth with a mug of soup.

Nick Nuttall - our club physio and all round good friend - rang to say the foot should get better with no running and plenty of rest. As it was going to be 30 miles a day for another three weeks the only answer was ICE.

I do admit to hiring Greg's spanner out for £5 to the charity, to a cyclist in distress. It's all business.

Peter is still searching for his crown jewels

Wednesday 2 May - Dumbarton - Chapelton Day 10

How did we get to here?

300 miles

This was a real turning point of the journey. We envisaged running for between five and six hours a day. That would be plenty hard enough. This was a hot day walking through dust and concrete after beautiful countryside. We walked all day until the light faded. I think this was a very dark time for Peter. He thought the time to throw in the towel was looming with so far still to go. But I also knew he would not give in, even if I ran and he walked, until he crossed the border back into England. Then he would at least have achieved the length of Scotland. Which in effect was nearly half of the total. I am sure Peter will have described the Clyde Tunnel in Glasgow. If not I can do it over a beer sometime. You pay and I say.

It was such a long day that we could not face the long drive to the campsite and then back again in the morning. So Greg just backed the van off the road into a clearing and sleep came easily.

Not even an earthquake could wake us tonight

Great placename of the day:
NETHER SKYBORRY
(Shropshire)
Wasn't he in Star Wars?

Running in honour of:
BRIAN HARLOW SMITH
1935 - 1995
Personal friend

Word of the day:
FESTOON
Decorate elaborately.

Quote for the day:
'Nothing succeeds like a toothless parrot.'
Anon

Day 11

330 miles

Thursday 3 May - Chapelton - Crawford

Old golden shoes is back

Great placename of the day:
OGBOURNE MAIZEY
(Wiltshire)
What a big girl, in all the right places.

Running in honour of:
ONGKAR ROBERT ANTHONY 'TONY' SMITH
1939 - 2006

The man with a great smile. Great organiser. Great worker for the Road Runner's Club. Founded the Sri Chinmoy 24 Hour Track Race. Started 'Run & Become' sport shop in 1982. I am glad that I crossed his path. My first marathon was 30 years ago today. Gillingham Marathon - 3.5.1982. I finished in 4 hours 7 minutes 42 seconds and said "never again". Total now - about 140!

Word of the day:
KERFUFFLE
A fuss or commotion.

Quote for the day:
'The running boy is inside every man, no matter how old he gets.'
Mitch Albom

What a difference a night makes. After a good sleep, practically on the start line, things looked very different. We found most days that we needed to start with a walk just to get the feet and legs into any gear and then hopefully into a nice tempo. Peter found that by changing his landing pattern he could beetle along quite well, but what would it be doing long-term? This did not really get mentioned as the focus was on finishing the day, thirty miles down the road. The payback time would come much later. Our physio Nick advised him to go as fast as possible to make a shorter day, allowing more time for icing and recovery. Hills were to be walked to avoid further pressure on the foot. It was a beautiful day with very warm sunshine in the afternoon.

A standing start

Friday 4 May - Crawford - Lockerbie   Day 12

The icing on the cake

360 miles

This was a good day, finishing at a lovely campsite. Greg bought chocolate fingers for Peter and bottles of beer for me. When I turned around the chocolate had disappeared and Peter was smiling very contentedly as if he had grown a new foot which functioned perfectly. This was my time to pull rank, age and anything else I have over him. It would not be good for him to demolish these boxes at such a rate. Rationing was called for although nothing was actually said. During the next few days while he was dozing with an ice-pack on his foot propped halfway up the wardrobe (I think he kept his slacks and smoking jackets in there) and I was preparing ham sandwiches with plain crisps inside, I would also place eight chocolate fingers on the plate as a garnish. How do you hide the remainder in a motorhome? I thought of sellotaping the box under the van as it would be too painful for Peter to get down there. But then I thought of one place he would never search. My beer stash was the perfect place and rationing continued.

He thinks I was funny reading every word, back and front, on the beer bottles, but not being an aficionado of imbibing how could he understand? The actual reason, apart from me being an annoying nerd, is that some beers are bottle-conditioned. This in technical terms means if you just pour it out as normal you will end up with an undrinkable pint of unpalatable cloudy liquid and two pounds gets poured down the drain. I have done this in the past and it hurts on many levels especially when it is the last bottle in the house and you have your beer head on. The beer is still fermenting in the bottle and this leaves bits and pieces at the bottom. So once you know you have one of these in your collection, great care needs to be used in the pouring process. That is why you read a beer label. Hello. Hello. Is anyone still out there?

Tomorrow we cross the border and get married by Greg at Gretna Green or the other way around actually!

Great placename of the day:
NEMPNETT THRUBWELL
(Avon)

Running in honour of:
'SEB' COE. BARON COE
Born 1956

Won four Olympic medals. He set eight outdoor and three indoor world records. Head of the London bid for the 2012 Olympics. They were incredible. A beautiful runner to watch.

Word of the day:
NINCOMPOOP
A simpleton. Nothing to do with him above.

Quote for the day:
'Time flies like an arrow. Fruit flies like a banana.'
Anthony Oethinger

Day 13 — Saturday 5 May - Lockerbie - St Cuthbert Without

390 miles

Peter's wife finds him a woman

Great placename of the day:

CLAXBY PLUCKACRE
(Lincolnshire)

Can be nasty if you get it in the nadgers.

Running in honour of:

YIANNIS KOUROS
Born 1956

Greek/Australian. Completed 303 kilometres in a 24 hour track race. This is amazing. Completed 1000 miles in 10 days 10 hours 30 minutes and 36 seconds. All time great at distance running.

Word of the day:

WONKY
Crooked. Unsteady.

Quote for the day:

'Hurrah for the squares entwinèd.'

As featured on the Blackheath Harriers badge. From the song of the Blackheath Harriers.

In the club magazine for March 1904.

A big day for many reasons. Peter had made it this far and was hoping for medical treatment to alleviate the foot problem. We went below 500 miles still to go. We crossed the border back into England in an angry mood, purely because of the sign. It was pathetic and dirty. We had obviously been holding out in our minds for something a little bit more Las Vegas style or at least some fairy lights and bunting.

Sue (Peter's wife) had scanned the internet and found someone willing to come to our campsite and heal the lame Peter. Kathryn, the 'Angel of the North' checked his foot, advised him that there was no fracture and showed him and Greg how to tape the foot up for the least damage as we continue our journey. I think I was either washing up, eating copious amounts of extremely hot home-made mustard pickle or reading my beer bottles again. It isn't good for me to go near technical things.

The border crossing that was well worth running a country for!?

134

Sunday 6 May - St Cuthbert Without - Fawcett Forest | Day 14

Trolling Up Hill

420 miles

'Shap' comes along just when you had something else planned. Everyone had mentioned this vast climb, so I think we had placed it at the back of our minds, that it would not bother us until the moment arrived. When Peter had gone to bed, some nights, I would have a beer with Greg and look in our large map book at where we would be travelling through the next day. We knew Shap was on the horizon, but not literally. On reaching the summit in sunshine I still felt my nose was going to drop off because of the cold air.

Nearing the highest point of the run...

then 'Trolling Down Hill' on the other side

Great placename of the day:

KINGSTON BAGPUIZE
(Oxfordshire)

Sounds like a very overweight cat.

Running in honour of:

LESLIE WATSON
Won London to Brighton race unofficially in 1979 and then officially in 1980. This was the early days of women running long distances. She had 68 marathon wins. She held the world best for 50 miles on the road. She was also glamorous and elegant. Sometimes I could even keep up with her.

Word of the day:

GUCK
Slimy matter.

Quote for the day:

'If you think you can do it, you're right. If you think you can't do it, you're still right.'
Henry Ford.

Day 15   **Monday 7 May - Fawcett Forest - Lancaster**

450 miles   Half full or half empty?

Great placename of the day:
CARLTON SCROOP
(Lincolnshire)

A money lender out of a Charles Dickens' novel.

Running in honour of:
GRETE WAITZ
1953 - 2011
Won New York Marathon 9 times. Won World Cross Country Championships 5 times. Held 3000m world record twice.

Word of the day:
GUBBINS
A set of equipment.

Quote for the day:
'Wisely and slow; they stumble that run fast.'
William Shakespeare. How wise he is.

Kendal was a nice place to celebrate the halfway point. But Peter's foot was raising its ugly head again. Can you say that? I think I just did. We were writing down injury clinic phone numbers, but all the time moving quite quickly away from where they were based. The words "cortisone injection" would be the most used that day. We had a lot of conflicting information, although everybody was trying to help. The bottom line seemed to be that if you have the injection you must rest for a couple of weeks and that was never going to happen.

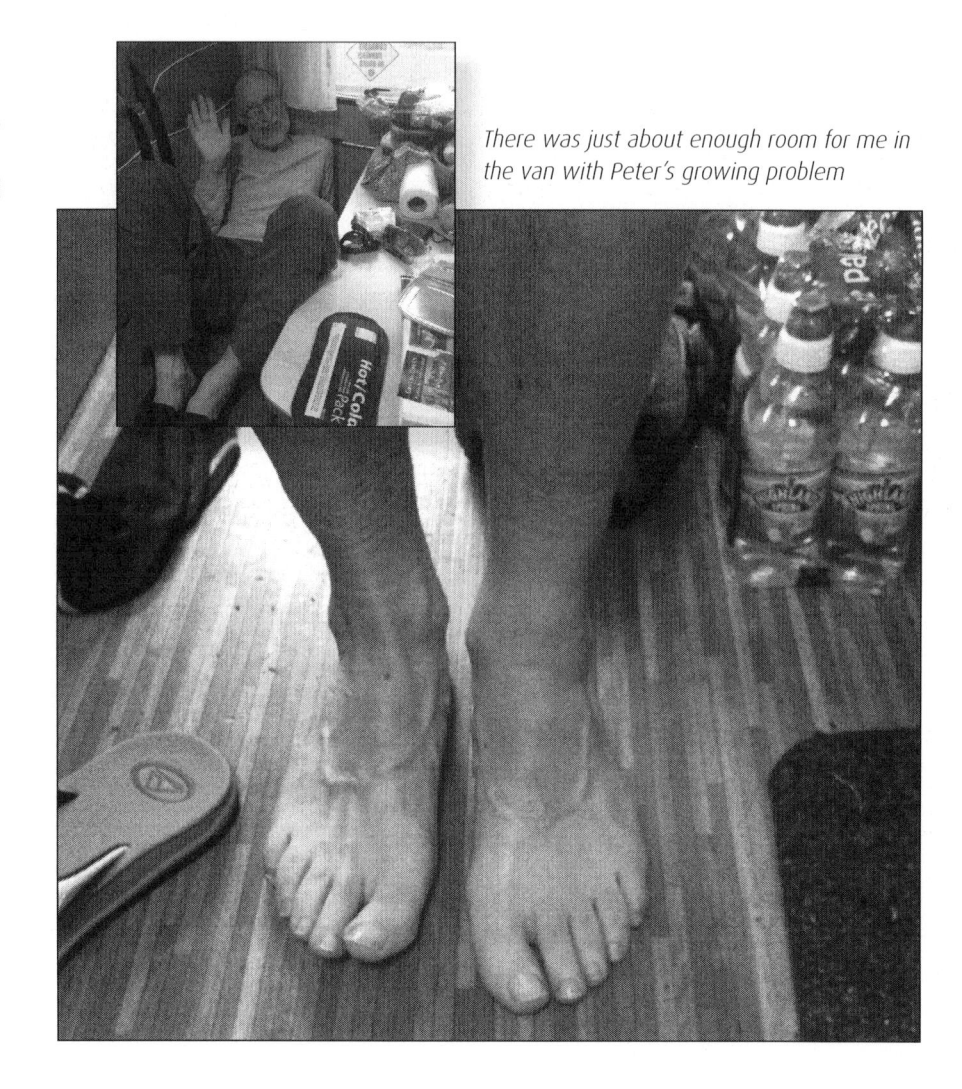

There was just about enough room for me in the van with Peter's growing problem

Tuesday 8 May - Lancaster - Euxton | Day 16

Long distance friends

480 miles

We had been concentrating so much on a few things that I think we were starting to go stir crazy. We awoke, got dressed, drank, ate, ran continuously throughout the days and I believe it was a very good idea when people (friends even) started to arrive. Although they cut across our daily rhythms they compensated in other ways. There was news from home and different subjects of conversation. There was often a present of some kind. Food parcels were brought as if we were under siege.

This day, Steve and Sharron Freemantle arrived having driven all the way from Norfolk! They stayed overnight so they could set us on our way again in the morning. The big long hug of a warm woman is an amazing thing when you have been away for awhile without it. Sorry, Peter and Greg, I know you tried your best but the stubble always gave you away.

Today we changed to four sessions of running and it seemed to help by getting more rests and more ice on Peter's foot.

The big long hug I was talking about

Great placename of the day:

BOOTHBY GRAFFOE
(Lincolnshire)

What do you get if you cross a giraffe with a bottle of gin?

Running in honour of:

'SMILER' SID MORRISON
Great competitor and race organiser. Not forgetting Mrs 'Sid'

Word of the day:

ARCHIPELAGO
Group of islands.

Quote for the day:

'Training is principally an act of faith.'
Franz Stampfl

Day 17

Wednesday 9 May - Euxton - Bartington

510 miles

A humbling experience

Great placename of the day:
SIXPENNY HANDLEY
(Dorset)
Elsie Tanner's real name. (I really am that old)

Running in honour of:
PAAVO NURMI
1897 - 1973
'The Flying Finn' 9 gold and 3 silver Olympic medals. 25 world records from 1500m to 20k.

Word of the day:
GUDDLE
To grope in water for fish.

Quote for the day:
'Diplomacy is thinking twice before saying nothing.'
Anon

I would like to be kind about the scenery on this day, but there wasn't any. We were the best looking things in Warrington as we passed the 500 miles run marker. Enough said.

The highlight of the day was when we went to the pub for a good meal, although we got soaked walking there. This is not true because we also met Mark Keyes. We were having a break in the van and it was raining quite steadily. We saw this person walking along with a huge pack on his back going in the opposite direction to us. We opened our door and asked if he would like to come in for a break. With him and his pack inside, the place was full. His pack, covered in very wet bin liners, I could just pick up a few inches from the floor. But he was carrying this all the way from Land's End to John O'Groats to raise money for Macmillan Cancer. He was carrying all he needed with him. We gave him food and drink and felt pretty humbled when he left us. There is always someone less fortunate etc.

The Mighty Mark

138

Thursday 10 May - Bartington - Quina Brook — **Day 18**

Leaving a good impression

540 miles

Today we were chaperoned through Whitchurch by Simon Parsons. He is another of the Blackheath Harriers who left behind the concrete jungle that is London. It did not look a dangerous place, in fact, it looked quite respectable, but you never know what goes on behind closed doors and Simon does live there. I think he knows the hostelries fairly well and so would I, in his shoes. He ran and met us a fair way out of town and would not say goodbye until we were well beyond the city limits on the other side. Maybe he was worried that these wild men, who had been running for two and a half weeks, would lower the tone of the place, where he is president of the local running club, Whitchurch Whippets. I am still waiting to be made an honorary life member and get my hands on some of their kit. Or possibly, he was worried about Greg and the local womenfolk.

Waiting at the campsite were my brother-in-law Lester and his wife Chris. It was a farmhouse with a lawn to the front. Although recently they had suffered a lot of rain, he told us to put our home up on the grass. As soon as we had parked we thought "how do we get it off here in the morning?" So we tried to get it back on the drive again, but the wheels span and we just made large muddy tracks in the grass. Lester is very practical and he was soon hitching us up to his vehicle and trying to pull us free. After a while the 'farmer' told us that he had

Simon, making sure we leave

Me pointing to Lester

Great placename of the day:
BRADFIELD COMBUST *(Suffolk)*
An early metal bra. It never really caught on.

Running in honour of:
SANDRA BROWN
Born 1949
Arguably the greatest ever female long distance walker. Did hold the record for Land's End to John O'Groats - 13 days and 10 hours.

Not forgetting husband Richard - another great walker.

Word of the day:
SCRUMPTIOUS
Delicious

Quote for the day:
'Fatigue's first victim is always one's sense of humour.'
James E Shapiro

Day 18 | **Cont/...**

Not sure who left the best impression - us on the lawn or the farmer on the drive?

a tractor and went around the back of the house to fetch it. Around the corner came an old vehicle, creaking and spluttering. He hitched us up to it (well the vehicle actually) and then drove off at breakneck speed. The slack on the rope disappeared, the tractor's front wheels started to rise and the back wheels made enormous craters in his driveway. I have the photos - very impressive. He did not seem to mind and we were back off his lawn and ready for the morning.

The facilities were a little spartan. Have you ever wondered what would happen to a bar of soap if you left it outside for twenty years? Well, we know the answer. We also met his mother who I think would have kept us there. Lester and Chris took me off to a pub for a lovely meal while Greg and Peter watched Top Gear. I never have liked those fashion programmes. When I came back neither of my friends had an axe in their head. Phew!

Friday 11 May - Quina Brook - Marshbrook | Day 19

Happy families

570 miles

Shrewsbury looked very nice in the sunshine. Later on Martyn Longstaff - who looks like his name - appeared with grandson Mark. He is another Blackheath runner. He had come up country to see his daughter and grandchildren and he hoped to run with us the next day. It was a day with a happy/sad ending. Maz (my wife) was driven over to see us by her schoolfriend Barbara and husband Michael. Guess where we went? Yes, a very nice pub restaurant. We were now getting used to this celebrity lifestyle and it was only the running that stopped us looking like Michelin men. The bad news was that I dropped a bag full of unopened beer bottles on the stone floor of the pub's entrance. Ale and tears spread a long way.

Outside the mother-ship with clubmate Martyn and his grandson Mark

I was far more interested in Maz than the menu

Great placename of the day:
HUISH CHAMPFLOWER
(Somerset)
Not sure what colour this is.

Running in honour of:
DON RITCHIE MBE
One of the greatest ultra-distance runners ever. In 1968 he ran 100k at Crystal Palace in 6 hours 10 minutes 20 seconds - a world record. John O'Groats to Land's End in 1989 - 10 days 15 hours 27 minutes.

Word of the day:
HIGHFALUTIN
Pretentious

Quote for the day:
'John Turner to tell you the truth,
Has done xxx marathons, struth.
But at the Paris race,
He fell flat on his face,
And now he's not so long in the tooth.'

Andy Tucker
Blackheath Harriers

Day 20 Saturday 12 May - Marshbrook - Wellington Marsh

600 miles

Surprise, surprise!

Great placename of the day:
BROUGHTON POGGS
(Oxfordshire)
I think I was in his older brother's class at Eton.

Running in honour of:
MELVILLE J BOUCHER
'Mev'
1926 - 2002
Personal friend

Word of the day:
VROOM
Roaring noise made by a motor vehicle.

Quote for the day:
'Peter Rogers he runs with our John
His stamina just goes on and on.
He ran the Comrades didn't he
Though no thanks to his kidney
And I think that his back's also gone.'
*Andy Tucker
Blackheath Harriers*

Ludlow looked very nice in the sunshine. Déjà vu for the second time. Later a car stopped and out climbed Martyn Longstaff in full club kit, to run with us for a while. I think Peter was doing three and I was doing two strides to match one of his. We met his family at the next stop. They were all so supportive of what we were doing. Our clubmates really made us very proud. I also know a lot of them wanted to see us at some point on our journey, but it was difficult when the nearest we came to London was Bristol!

We were just settling back into our routine when Mike Peel and Terri Shotton arrived. These lovely friends do an amazing amount of work for our club. They truly are a part of its backbone, holding everything together. Mike had his kit with him, of course, and ran with us while Terri attempted to take photos by whizzing past us in her new car, dashing out and clicking away. I think she had a lovely set of tree and sky pictures. They stayed at our campsite so - shall we all chant it together - we went to a pub for a meal!

Here we are at 600 miles completed.

Peter, Mike, Lord Gaga, the Red Ball, Greg and Terri

Sunday 13 May - Wellington Marsh - Llandogo — Day 21

Room for one more...

630 miles

Long distance running is beginning to have an effect on me...

Hereford looked very nice in the sunshine. Our physio Nick Nuttall arrived to stay with us for a couple of days. Not in the van, but even better. More of this later.

Nick stayed for dinner at the campsite. He then massaged Peter in the gent's toilet. I hope we are after the watershed and all the children are tucked up safely. I tell you no lies, just read into it whatever you like. Greg went to the other side of the field to help a 'Simon' put up his yurt. I thought I would have a little bit of quiet reflection and take the fluff out of my navel when there was a knock at the door. It was just like the first Christmas - I know, I'm that old! Standing outside in the fading light were Madonna and child saying they needed somewhere warm. I said, 'had they tried Majorca?' - 'It's meant to be cheap as well.' Just to re-cap it was only the mother who said she wanted to share my pad. The baby only said "goo-goo" type things. I do like accuracy even while writing this drivel. They were Erica and baby Rugi, the other part of 'Yurt Simon's' family. They had been sent over in the cool gloom until the structure had been completed. I was just entertaining them when there was another knock on the door. Is this how Woodstock started? Valerie came in as she had seen our posters on the van and wanted to donate to the charity. Peter and Greg returned to a cosy little party.

Great placename of the day:

AINDERBY QUERNHOW
(North Yorkshire)
Can you rearrange to make a well known phrase or saying?

Running in honour of:

DEAN KARNAZES
Born 1962
50 marathons in 50 states in 50 days. Etc... say no more. An animal of the running world.

Word of the day:

JETTISON
Throw overboard.

Quote for the day:

'We run because we like it,
Through the broad bright land.'

*Charles Hamilton Sorley
1895 - 1915
From 'the Song of the Ungirt Runners'*

Day 22

Monday 14 May - Llandogo - Yanley

660 miles

Finally, I did something right

Great placename of the day:

COMPTON PAUNCEFOOT *(Somerset)*
An injury my friend Mark was struck down with.

Running in honour of:

ALICE BILLSON
A little everybody's granny with white hair. Ran along waving and smiling. A great example of the joy of running. She ran the Croydon 10k in April 2000. She finished ahead of six people and was in the race as a veteran woman over 55 years old. She was 87 years young at the time! Bless her, wherever she may be.

Word of the day:

SERENDIPITY
Happy discovery by accident.

Quote for the day:

'Choose your running companions very carefully. In my experience, deaf mutes are a good bet. More runners die from boredom every year than through heart attacks and road accidents combined.'

Andy Blackford

This was the day of the big right turn. Like we had planned and dreamed of crossing the border from Scotland back into England this was the other big event we had on the horizon. Cross the Severn Bridge which is very long and then make sure you turn right towards Cornwall.

Nick had booked himself into the very up-market Avon Gorge Hotel. He just needed to know how to find it. It's restaurant looked out on the Clifton Suspension Bridge, but with the pouring rain, curved hilly roads and one-way streets it was difficult to locate. I used the bath while Peter went on the massage table Nick had set up at the bottom of his bed. If people had come in with a camera at specific moments it could have looked quite dodgy. But we are all married and we were lonely. Nick then treated us to a very fine meal. Guilty conscience I suppose. Only joking. I can feel the lawsuits being taken out of the wardrobe. Get it. I know I will in a minute, if anybody bothers to read this stuff.

I'm actually indicating our right turn, not thumbing a lift

Physio Nick with last minute instructions for Peter before we start

144

Tuesday 15 May - Yanley - Bridgwater | Day 23

More trolling...

690 miles

Unbelievable, but we have under 200 miles to go. We ran a long second section which meant just two short legs to finish the day. They obviously belong to Peter.

After 690 miles two locals, Peter & Paul, point us in the direction of the local Social Care Trust

Great placename of the day:
BURTON COGGLES
(Lincolnshire)
Now I know why he wears glasses.

Running in honour of:
WALTER GOODALL GEORGE
1858 - 1943
Blackheath Harrier. In 1886 he ran a new record for one mile - 4 minutes 12¾ seconds. This record lasted for almost 30 years.

Word of the day:
PANTECHNICON
Large van.

Quote for the day:
'If you think you are a runner, get out and run! And enjoy it! I do.'
Bruce Tulloh

| Day 24 | Wednesday 16 May - Bridgwater - Tiverton |

720 miles

Making the most of it

Great placename of the day:

ASTON FLAMVILLE
(*Leicestershire*)
The names that they give cars these days.

Running in honour of:

FAUJA SINGH
Born 1911
He moved to Britain in the 1960s. He took up running after his wife and son died. He holds the incredible record of 5 hours 40 minutes for running the marathon aged over 90. At 100 years old he finished the Toronto Waterfront Marathon in Canada, with a time under 8½ hours. Also at age 100 he ran 5k in 38 minutes 34 seconds.

Word of the day:

HUNKY-DORY
Very satisfactory.

Quote for the day:

'The tongue weighs practically nothing, but so few people can hold it.'
Anon

Sometimes, things just happen. We have been in a sort of routine for ages and then because of a series of errors we strike lucky. We missed the turning and the van so we had to have a coffee break in an Asda supermarket. We were happy enough as the coffee was real, the sandwiches were made for us and Peter could get a bag of peas out of the freezer for his foot.

Later we came to the welcome to Devon sign. Just two more counties to cross. They are both quite large and very hilly. We still thought that we were running the country the best way. The finish at John O'Groats would not have appealed to us.

Thursday 17 May - Tiverton - Okehampton | Day 25

Beginning to feel the miles

750 miles

Day twenty-five. As I levered my body down from the top bunk bed I remember thinking to myself that I felt tired for the first time and maybe it is just as well that there are only a few days to go. Before we set off from John O'Groats I expected to say I was tired about day four. So my body held out well for another three weeks. I do also remember Greg climbing over a barbed wire fence in his shorts to get a photograph of a field of grass. He was right because it is a great picture.

Greg demonstrating the benefits of stretching

Great placename of the day:

DIBDEN PURLIEU *(Hampshire)*
A special knitting stitch where you use three needles.

Running in honour of:

SIR JOHN GEORGE WALKER KNZM CBE
Born 1952
First to run the one mile in under 3 minutes 50 seconds. 1976 - Gold medal in Olympic 1500m

1985. First to run 100 sub 4 minute mile races.

Total of 135 mile races under 4 minutes.

1996. Announced he was suffering from Parkinson's. Beautiful to watch in full flight.

Word of the day:

PARAPHERNALIA
Miscellaneous belongings.

Quote for the day:

'Never look down on anybody unless you're helping them up.'
Jesse Jackson

147

Day 26

780 miles

Friday 18 May - Okehampton - St Ive

Better 'mad' than 'sad' men*

Great placename of the day:

BLUBBERHOUSES
(North Yorkshire)
But should be in Wales?

Running in honour of:

THE SARGEANTS.
PETER AND MRS LEO
Great supporters of running. Especially the ultra end of the sport. Peter was the oldest finisher in the London to Brighton race 5 times. Although getting older they still do marshalling and lap counting. Leo makes the wonderful and famous ultra cake to hand out at races.

Word of the day:

PUSILLANIMOUS
Timid.

Quote for the day:

'Adventure is worthwhile in itself.'
Amelia Earhart

*From the second verse of the 'Song of the Blackheath Harriers.'

Tomo, you are still the man. I think they put the moulds together when they made you. Months before, back in the planning stages, he had said that if he was around he would bagpipe us over the border from Devon into Cornwall. This was achieved in great style. Peter and I were running down this painfully steep hill when through the wind in the overhanging trees you could hear some music. I thought someone must have been driving their car along the road at the bottom with their windows open. But no, it was Tomo standing in the middle of the old stone bridge over the River Tamar that constitutes the border. He played lustily in his Blackheath Harriers adapted Scottish regalia while we ran up an equally steep hill, wait for it, to a pub. I thought I had finished for the day and ordered a beer. Not a great idea when we had to set off again. If you want very hilly roads to run on, look no further than Devon and Cornwall. Scotland, in my mind, had high peaks, but the roads we went on mainly went around rather than up and over. Tomo also kept arriving with strawberries and giant pasties. Cornish of course.

Campsites go like most things from the sublime to the ridiculous. A couple we stayed at had obviously not been inspected recently and should have been closed down. Others were spartan but were clean enough and had all that we needed. Then there were the ones that you just wanted to stay at. Either the setting in the scenery or the fantastic people and sometimes you got both. Our hostess on this evening said that our stay would be free and that she would bring us a cream tea over to the van. There was a knock at the door at about 8.30pm and Kathryn stood there with a tray covered with a tea-towel. When we lifted the cover it was poetry. We had obviously been accepting that nothing will be that fancy when you have three men stuck in a van for almost a month. There were china cups, saucers and plates piled up, milk in a jug, a teapot full of amber nectar (no not lager) and a plate overloaded with large scones, butter, cream and jam. We were made to feel very special. Thank you so much Fursdown Farm.

Saturday 19 May - St Ive - Grampound | Day 27

The rest is history

810 miles

It was a much warmer day today. How do I know this? Each day without really thinking, as you just get into a rhythm of repetition, I had been putting four layers on my top half and two layers on my lower. We could definitely go out with less today. We love the freedom of running just in vest and shorts but it had not been dry or warm enough for this. I think we also overcompensated to ensure our health stayed at the best level possible. The camping chairs we had bought had never been out of their cases. So when we took our second break we lounged in luxury outside in the warm sunshine. It felt therapeutic to our now jaded bodies. Ah!

As we ran near St. Austell we saw the Olympic Torch Relay coming the other way. We had just reached a roundabout so we stopped to enjoy the spectacle.

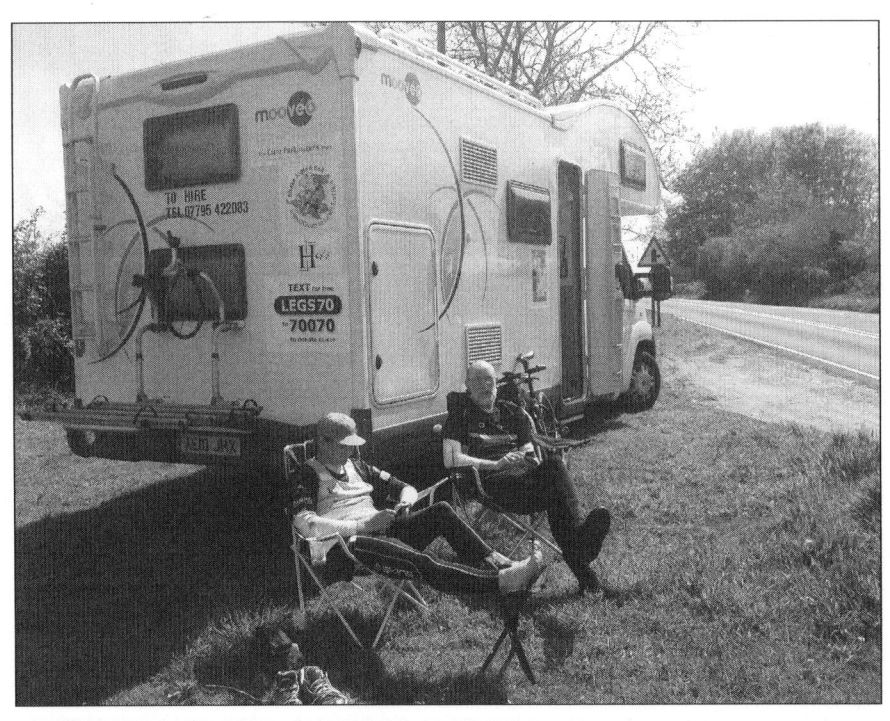

It seemed a shame to bring the chairs all this way and not use them

Great placenames of the day:

DIRT POT
(Northumberland)
NEWTON BLOSSOMVILLE
(Buckinghamshire)
TIPTOE
(Hampshire)
SWAY
(Hampshire)
SPLATT
(Cornwall)

Running in honour of:

GEOFF OLIVER
Now aged 79 and about to run in yet another 24 hour track race. Broke first world record when aged 65. He holds the world best for 24 hours on the track aged over 75 years of 111 miles, Quite incredible.

Word of the day:

SPOFFISH
Fussy.

Quote for the day:

When asked his religion in hospital Woody Guthrie said:
"All or none."

149

Day 28

Sunday 20 May - Grampound - Ashton

840 miles

Steaming towards the finish

Great placenames of the day:
MANKINHOLES
(West Yorkshire)
DRAYTON PARSLOW
(Buckinghamshire)
LYTCHETT MATRAVERS
(Dorset)

Running in honour of:
Catherine (Kay) O'Regan and Mr Joe, Geoff Hoggett, Tony and Maureen Farmer, Dan Coffey, Ian Champion, Don Turner, Pam Storey, Paul Watts, James Zarie, Jim Bailey, Roy Parris, Gil John, Mike Hawthorne, Ron Hill, Edwin Bartlett, Harry Martin, Brian 'the Ladders' Doherty and Mrs, Roger Biggs, all the Farts and Wednesday Nighters, Tarit Adrian Stott, Shankara Smith and family and all the Sri Chinmoy people, Ann Bath, Dave Leal, Helen Stephen, John Clarke.

Word of the day:
JIGGERY-POKERY
Trickery.

Quote for the day:
'You only live once, but if you work it right, once is enough.'
Joe Louis

Just fifty miles left to run. We were steaming up a hill when a traction engine started to steam down the hill. We had to stop and have a chat and a photo. All silly chuffers together.

Later in the day, after some strenuous hills, we were having our break when Maz and Helen arrived with coffee and cakes. All we now wanted to see was our first road sign saying Land's End - so many miles to go. But I think they have taken them out so people don't get too excited and ruin their nearly completed adventure. When Greg said we could finish for the day there was a milestone showing 17 miles to go. Hardly worth getting up for tomorrow. But we knew it would be far enough in reality.

In the evening, we met up with Maz and Helen again, who had taken accommodation nearby, and had a lovely meal together.

Full steam ahead - in both directions!

Monday 21 May - Ashton - Land's End — Day 29

On the threshold of a dream

854.8 miles

Nothing had prepared us for this final day. It felt and looked like the final scene from a blockbuster film. The scenery, weather, emotion and music all came together for a memorable finale.

We had seventeen or eighteen miles remaining and it felt very strange. A bit like slow motion action. Peter had told me a couple of weeks into the run that an anonymous donor was willing to give £50 to the charity if I arrived at the finish clean shaven. The problem was trying to find somewhere open at a convenient time to fit our running and breaks. It had still not been achieved and we were running out of space and time. It was a gloriously hot sunny day as we ran down into Penzance, which I know quite well from previous holidays. As we ran up the High Street Greg pointed us into a barber shop while he went off, still attending to all our needs, to get coffee and cakes. The lovely Leah shaved me good and proper so we knew the money for Cure Parkinson's was in the bag. She filled up our water bottles and said she had done the cutting for free.

Tomo kept appearing and disappearing every few miles always with his bagpipes and camera. He was giving us last minute panics with his tactics. These Cornish peninsular roads are narrow and winding enough for tired runners to negotiate, but when you add Tomo driving slowly along on the wrong side of the road, leaning out of his window taking pictures whilst steering with his knees, I thought all three of us would leave this planet at the same time in a spectacular crash!

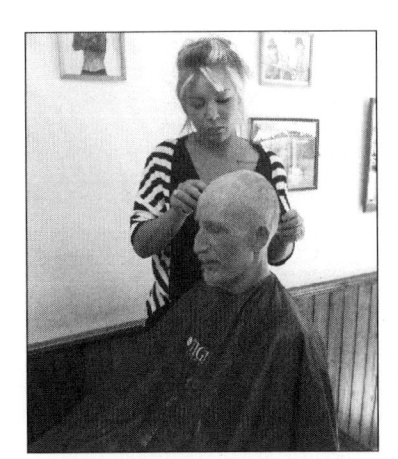

What some people will do for £50!

Great placenames of the day:

ROSEBERRY TOPPING
(Border of Cleveland & North Yorkshire)
MARSTON TRUSSELL
(Northamptonshire)
FICKLESHOLE
(Surrey)

Running in honour of:

ARTHUR NEWTON
1883 - 1959
Won Comrades Marathon 5 times. In 1928 broke the 100 mile record on the Bath to London road. 14 hours 22 minutes and 10 seconds. He became professional and broke the same course 100 mile record in 1934. 14 hours 6 minutes. Aged 51.

Word of the day:

UGGLESOME
Horrible.

Quote for the day:

'Nothing great is easy.'
Epitaph of Captain Matthew Webb. The first person to swim the English Channel. 1875.

Day 29 — Cont/...

We took our last break with just 4 miles to go. We were going to savour these moments after being on the road for a month. As we headed off into the corner that makes Cornwall a triangle, the sea was beautiful on both sides in the sunshine. We came over the last hill and could hear again the sound of bagpipes. Tomo was at the finish orchestrating a grand finale. Also at the finish line were Greg, Maz, Helen, coach loads of excited Japanese tourists and a few locals who wondered what all the fuss was about.

It was fitting that Greg, who had done everything to make this dream come true, had finished in first place. Peter and I jumped the line together to take the equal runner-up position. Peter is the 'champagne' man to my beer preference. But on this occasion I was ready to celebrate with the bubbly stuff. So what happens? Greg decides to treat us like the drivers on the podium after a Formula One Grand Prix. I end up running around the car park adding junk miles to our total while he soaks my best Blackheath Club kit with very sticky alcohol. We had our official finish photographs taken and then went inside to sign in, that we had ended our journey.

Sitting on this rocky final piece of mainland South West England, looking out towards America, it felt very special. We should never take our legs for granted. Mobility is almost everything.

We are going to celebrate with our tired bodies tonight. We go to the nearest pub and try to stay awake. We sit there, Maz, Helen, Greg, Peter and I under a ceiling full of vests proclaiming other great journeys for charity. We arrange for us to share these dizzy heights. Then Peter had an accident with a couple of bottles of strong red wine. He drank them. Anyone wishing to know what happened next must have a fat cheque book. For only I know the lurid details!

Also running in honour of:

All my daughters, real and otherwise, Claire, Zoë, Amy, Zita, Anita, Rowan and Cathy. My in-laws Fred and Lore Stuart. My grandchildren Tatiana, George, Thomas, Ellie and Daniel. All the Hayes Family. Dr David Corbett and staff at the Orchard Practice, Dartford. Nick Nuttall, Tomo and his pipes. The Cure Parkinson's Trust and everybody from our clubs and the great British public. It seems so long ago now but we must not forget Alison Smith and the John O'Groats area folk that saw us off on what was to become a successful venture in so many, many ways.

Tony Hawks, Sharon Gayter, Tom Isaacs, Caroline Leal, Les Roberts, Tony Pontifex, Steve Hollingdale, Anne Cilia, Mark Ellison, Roy Poultney, Steve & Nida Fletcher, Gerald, Iain, Eva & Lennard, Kyara, Bronwyn & Michael, Angela, my sister Jan and husband Jon, their daughter Carly and all other family everywhere. Lots of thanks to Sue Rogers, Ben and Maff and their girlfriends. Blackheath & Bromley Triathlon section, I salute you for your help with fund raising.

Snippets 1

We must take our hats off to Eddie Wright. I believe it was in 1994 that he ran from John O'Groats to Land's End. He not only ran it on his own but it rained on 26 of his 28 days. Enough said.

Whilst following Peter's footsteps at about mile 764.2, I tripped on a lump of stone at the edge of the road. On my way down and just as I was about to stick my head up the wheel arch of a passing Land Rover, Peter pushed me away into the undergrowth. Never try to get out of anything when doing it with a friend!

The three things I was most worried about were:

Blisters. I did not get a single one

The weather. We were very lucky indeed.

Greg. Because he is Australian. But we were let off lightly because he is a Tasmanian.

Snippets 2

Peter likes a good schedule to follow but he has to have what I give him.

I started putting a £2 coin away every day from 10/10/2010. This helped to finance the mission without feeling it so much.

I asked Maz on 10/3/2011 if it would be possible for me to go with Peter for a run lasting a month. She said "Yes".

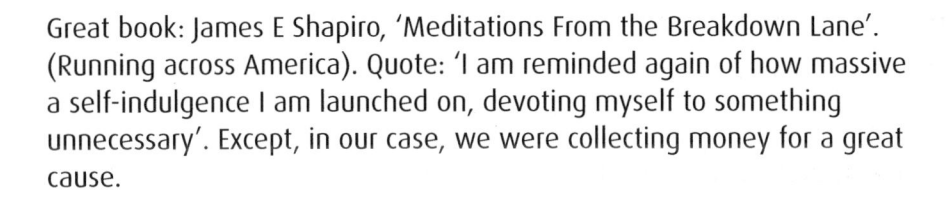

Great book: James E Shapiro, 'Meditations From the Breakdown Lane'. (Running across America). Quote: 'I am reminded again of how massive a self-indulgence I am launched on, devoting myself to something unnecessary'. Except, in our case, we were collecting money for a great cause.

Paradoxically I found LOSTWITHIEL (Cornwall) was my favourite place that we ran through.

Snippets 3

One of the best physio stories ever.

Peter contacted Nick, one of our club physios, when he needed help for his foot. Nick said the best thing would be to immerse the foot in a bucket of ice. So Peter started doing this to his foot until it turned a bit bluish after an hour.

After a few days Nick rang to check on his patient and asked if Peter had noticed any improvement after icing his foot. Peter said that he had. Nick said it was amazing, how after four or five minutes the benefit could be felt. Did we or maybe it was only I that laughed a lot. Peter had only multiplied the treatment between twelve and fifteen times. Always remember to ask the question, "How long do I do this for?" But maybe the Rogers' method will now get into the textbooks.

Snippets 4

It all kicked off at Easter just as we reached the crucial long training weekend. 6th April 2012. Good Friday. All the months of preparing had gone well and it only remained to complete three days of the actual schedule, before we started to taper off our training. 24.7 miles in 4 hours and 1 minute. Very good. But afterwards the whole of my chest area felt bruised and tender. Try not to panic and see what it is like in the morning. It was no better. On the Sunday morning it was still the same so I told Peter to carry on without me. As it was Easter weekend the surgery was closed. Luckily on the Tuesday Maz got me an appointment with my own doctor. This is good as he has run the London Marathon. I see him on Wednesday 11th April and tell him what hurts and what we are about to undertake. He said it was most probably going to get better within a few days but it was best to check everything out. He asked me to come back at the end of the day for an E.C.G. and return on the Friday 13th at 8am for a host of blood tests. This was a whole week without running a step!

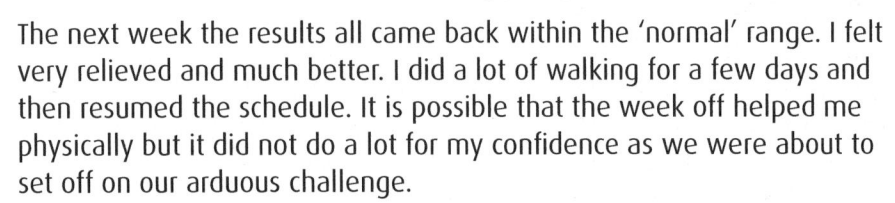

The next week the results all came back within the 'normal' range. I felt very relieved and much better. I did a lot of walking for a few days and then resumed the schedule. It is possible that the week off helped me physically but it did not do a lot for my confidence as we were about to set off on our arduous challenge.

This is definitely going to be my final comment. Honest. If it was not for Maz, I am sure that I would have been a wandering alcoholic, a man of the roads. Most probably 'Forrest Gumping' the John O'Groats to Land's End route many times.

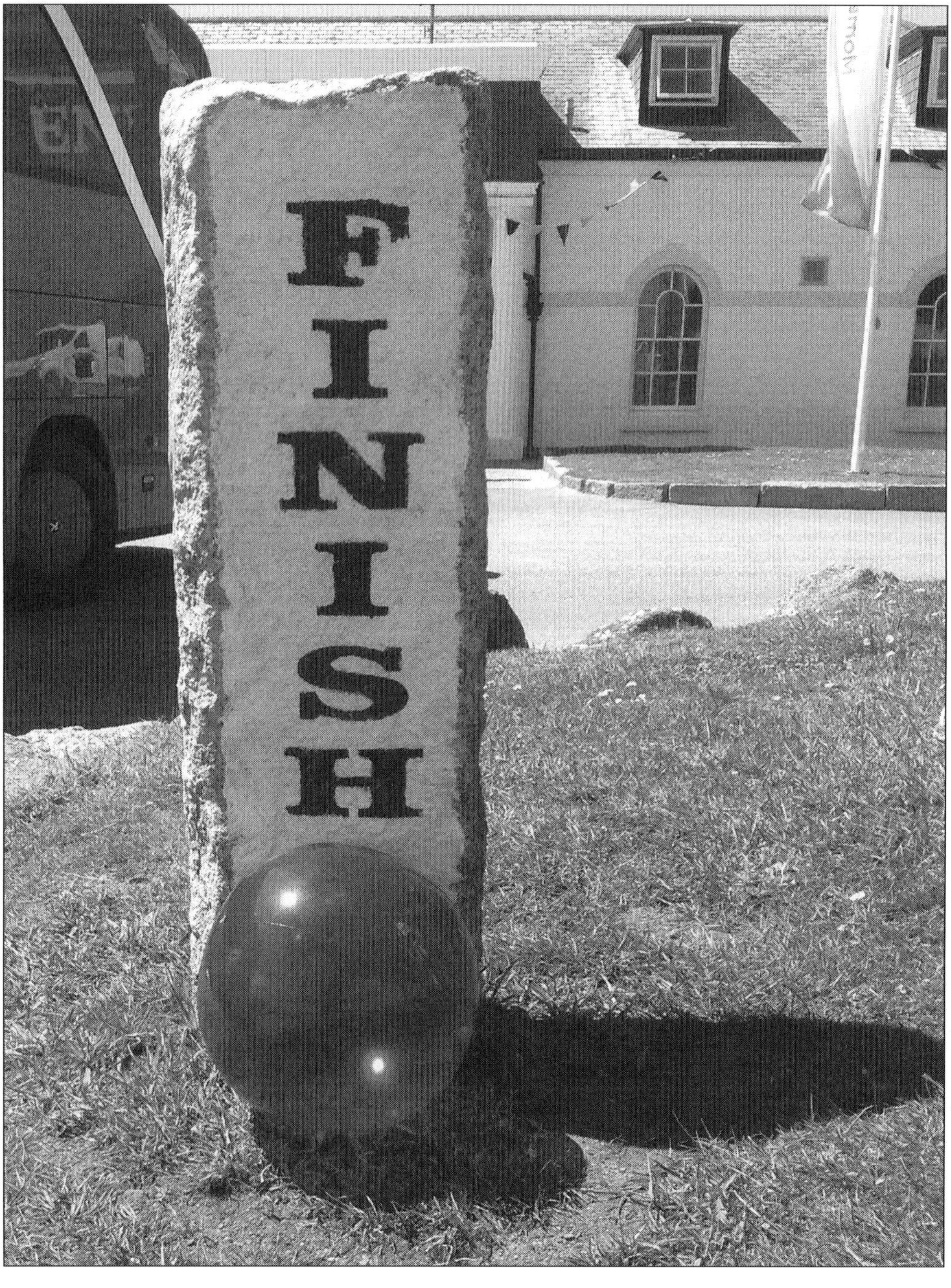
FINISH

Who said staying at home was easy?
(Acrostic)

Just one month away is all I ask. Please can I go?
Only if you buy a mobile phone is my reply.
How was I to know there would be days without a signal.
Never thought it would worry me so.

Organise my month of freedom.

Great to have time to myself, I think,
Reading and knitting late into the night.
Offer to help with London Marathon baggage,
At end of day fall into bed exhausted.
The grandchildren keep me busy: lots of laughs.
Sleepovers with family and friends make the time pass.

Theatre with friends and a Super Spring Clean.
Off to meet John at Little Stretton via friends in Kidderminster.

Look forward to Sutton Park relays and a stay with my bro' near Stafford
And there's the Kent Vets league meetings with Blackheath and Bromley.
Not long now but I'm feeling lonely, although I'm not alone.
Devon and Cornwall are calling: 19th May set off with Helen.
See cricket match near Dorchester then stay with a friend in Strete.

Excellent hostel accommodation for Sunday and Monday near Sennen.
Now we're at Land's End to greet the heroes with the bagpipes playing!
Did I miss John? Of course I did!!!

Maz Turner

Some helpful reading

I read a great many books whilst researching and preparing our Jogle challenge. These are some of the most useful. One book won't solve all your problems, but there is something to learn from each of the books listed here.

Special mention
From Wits' End to John O'Groats
Les Roberts
The amusing account of a fellow club member's End-to-End bike ride in aid of the Cure Parkinson's Trust

End to End Accounts

Where does that footpath lead? The story of one woman's run from Land's End to John O'Groats
Carole Loader

Hairy McNair's Humongous Hobble - Land's End to John O'Groats in 18 days
Robert Hall-McNair

The Clock Keeps Ticking - An amazing long journey into the life of Great Britain's top ultra runner (includes a chapter on her LeJog run)
Sharon Gayter

End to End
Steve Blease

A Journey of Soles - Land's End to John O'Groats
Kathy Trimmer

End to End Guides

Land's End to John O'Groats - Cycle Guide
Simon Brown

John O'Groats to Land's End - The official challenge guide
A walkers guide
Brian Smailes

Land's End to John O'Groats - A choice of footpaths for walking the length of Britain
Andrew McCloy

Training/Fitness/Nutrition Guides

The Complete Guide to Sports Nutrition - How to eat for maximum performance
Anita Bean

Endurance Sports Nutrition - Eating plans for optimal training, racing and recovery
Suzanne Girard Eberle, MS, RD

Fixing your Feet - Injury prevention and treatments for athletes
John Vonhof

Running Injury-Free - How to prevent, treat and recover from dozens of painful problems
Joe Ellis, D.P.M, with Joe Henderson

Training for Ultras
Edited by Andy Milroy

50 50 - Secrets I learned running 50 marathons in 50 days - and how you too can achieve super endurance!
Dean Karnazes with Matt Fitzgerald

Everyman's Guide to Distance Running
Norrie Williamson

Lore of Running - Discover the Science and Spirit of Running
Tim Noakes, MD

Inspirational

And then the vulture eats you - True tales about ultra marathons and those who run them
Edited by John L Parker, Jr.

Ultra Marathon Man - Confessions of an all-night runner
Dean Karnazes

Life on the run: Coast to Coast
Matt Beardshall

The Extra Mile : One Woman's Personal Journey to Ultra-Running Greatness
Pam Reed

Wild Trails to Far Horizons: Ultra-distance Runner
Mike Cudahy and John Beatty

Just a little run around the world: 5 years, 3 packs of wolves and 53 pairs of shoes
Rosie Swale Pope

Shake Well Before Use - A walk Around Britain's Coastline
Tom Isaacs

DVDs

78 days 2659 miles The Ultimate Marathon Man - Scotland to the Sahara
Andrew Murray

Land's End to John O'Groats - A Cyclists Guide
The Story of a cycle ride from Land's End to John O'Groats - the route, what to eat, how to prepare and what to take.

A few useful APPs

Other APPs are available! But these are some of the APPs that we found most useful.

I am a dedicated Apple Mac user in daily life but didn't want to take my Mac on the road with me so sought to do all that I could via the iPhone. Greg used both an iPhone and an iPad throughout the event.

A word of warning: finding a signal (we were both on O2) was not always easy and on two occasions we were unable to upload the blog until the following morning.

Navigation

Maps and **Google Maps** - useful for confirming exact position, piloting through towns and dropping pins so that you can follow a route.

MapMyRun - Complete route plotting and following. Highly recommended.

Find Friends - Very useful for handler to locate runners and runners to locate the van.

Strava Run - Turns the iPhone into a Garmin! Tracks distance, speed, splits and calories plus elevation. For best result should be used with Bad Elf GPS, see below (The current version is not 100% accurate over distance so not perfect for accurate measurement of LeJog)

Bad Elf GPS - Boosts Satellite reception, but it does use a lot of power so needs careful management for very long runs - also quite expensive.

National Cycle Network - Brilliant free APP showing the whole network (25,000 miles across the UK). Useful for finding traffic free or quieter routes.

Compass - Does what it says on the tin!

RAC Traffic+ - Up to the minute traffic updates and information.

Accommodation

Sites UK - Over 3000 UK sites. Multi search options.

C&C Guide - Multi search option including GPS enabled. Site Info stored in APP.

Tesco Finder - Tescos will allow free overnight campervan camping in their carparks, but conditions apply and it's best to make contact with the store manager (and perhaps buy something!).

England BB - Official Tourist Guide for B&Bs. This was a back up in case we needed the unplanned comfort of a B&B and needed to find the nearest one.

Communication

OffExploring - Great blogging site that can be linked directly to Facebook and Twitter which is very useful when time is precious. Also possible to order the blog as a hardback or paperback book when finished.

Facebook - Just another reminder how useful the iPhone is if you don't want to be tied to your computer.

Twitter - Found this one particularly useful when needing help!

Flickr - I set it up, but we didn't use this in the end but many have to organise photos for such events.

iLoader - Easy way to upload pictures to multiple sites.

Voice Memos - Useful for recording information when typing is not possible.

General

Sports Injury Clinic and **First Aid** - Worth having out on the road.

Met Office - For accurate weather updates.

iSearch and **AroundMe** - Useful for finding local amenities (pubs, shops, petrol stations etc).

Pages - A word processing APP that you can use to write up the day and have available on your computer when you get home.

AutoStitch - My favourite, favourite APP. Check it out!

Another valuable use of the iPhone was as a substitute map. If the route was simple and I didn't want to carry the Landranger or Section sheet I took a photo of it so that I could refer to it in case of emergency. I could also take a photo of other information we might need.

A useful website

The Land's End John O'Groats Association
www.landsend-johnogroats-assoc.com
A wealth of information for anyone considering or planning an End to End adventure.

Running kit (the basics)

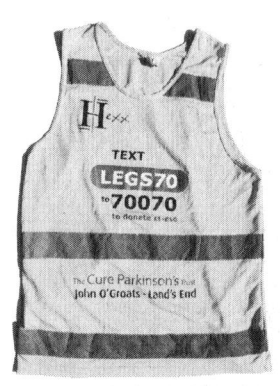

4 pairs of running shoes (change at each break)
1 pair of oversized running shoes (to allow for swelling)
6 pairs of lycra shorts
2 pairs compression tights (option to wear 1 pair at night)
2 pairs compression gaiters (so socks can be changed)
2 large Hi-viz running vests (to wear over kit)
8 pairs Falke F3 socks (change every break to avoid blisters)
8 pairs underpants
6 technical running T shirts
6 technical long sleeve running shirts
1 hi-viz Climafit cap (keep wind and rain out of the face)
1 thin woolly hat
1 thicker woolly hat
1 pair dark glasses
1 warm waterproof/windproof Jacket
1 light waterproof/windproof Jacket
1 light running jacket
2 high viz vests
1 pair comfortable slippers
1 pair flip-flops
1 warm jumper

Garmin watch (to monitor time, distance and pace)
iPhone (communication, navigation and information)
Waterproof iPhone arm band (to keep hands free)
Waterproof map case
Lights (that can be fixed to clothing)

Medical & Foot Care kit

Kool Pak - instant ice packs
Sports hot/cold compress
Recoverice - Ice Wrap bandage
Deep Freeze cold spray
Deep Heat Spray
Ibuprofen gel
Fabric Elastoplast
Strappal 5cm x 5m tape
Fortuna Zinc Oxide Tape
10cm x 3.2m Ijsverband
Compeed
Savlon Blister Plasters
Anti-Blister stick
Soft tubular bandage
Corn Wraps
Foot Cream (for dry, hard skin)
Sudocream
Pro Sport elasticated ankle support
Pro Sport elasticated knee support

Heel Pain relief orthotic
Rehydration sachets
Eurax cream - anti itching cream
Savlon Antiseptic Cleansing Wipes
Savlon Antiseptic Cream
Savlon Antiseptic Wound Wash
First Defence - protective hand gel
Arnicare - arnica cream for bruises
Aspirin
Paracetamol
Ibuprofen
Digital thermometer
Space blanket
P20 10hr factor 20 sun protection
Vaseline
Emery boards
Nail scissors / tweezers
Needle
Lighter

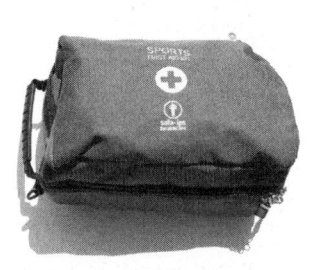

ULTRAstore - Footcare Pack
1 Tincture Benzoin tape adherent in brush applicator bottle
1 metre Hapla tape 2.5 cm
1 metre Hapla tape 5 cm
50cm Hapla tape 7 cm
2 x ID silicon lube sachets
10cm fleecy web padded tape
10cm Optiflex second skin transparent tape
2 x no 11 scalpel blades - sterile and individually wrapped
1 container of Zeazorb powder (7 x more absorbent than normal talc)
1 x pad fleecy foam self adhesive padding
3 x duct tape squares for extreme blister cover when roof of blister has been lost
Gauze swabs
4 x cutisoft IPA alcohol wipes single use

From Rory Coleman's ULTRAstore

Everything you need in one handy pack to fix a multitude of foot problems. Excellent for multiday events. Comes with an information sheet describing how to use each of the items.

www.ultrarace.co.uk/catalogue

Our take on Nutrition

This is an interesting one. Although important it was the one area of research that really didn't turn me on. Having read the books and articles, combed the internet and talked to those with experience we probably didn't follow that much of the advice! Whilst training we experimented with food on the go - peanut butter and jam sandwiches, crisps, chocolate raisins, bananas, coffee, water and Lucozade sport. But after a few days on the run it became clear that we needed to eat what we felt like eating during the day - which turned out to be ham salad sandwiches, fruit bars, crisps and coffee with water or Lucozade for the run. And then in the evening a pile of pasta and rice and noodles.

For the first few days I found it very hard to physically eat enough. I've always found it easy to eat 15-20 minutes after a long run but then the window closes and my stomach doesn't want to receive anything for 2-3 hours. This wasn't practical for us so Greg had chips or garlic bread ready for us as soon as we finished which we could munch on while driving to the campsite.

While we showered and changed Greg put our kit in to wash and then cooked stir-fry or pasta bake or spaghetti or on a couple of occasions - steak!

I avoided desserts as too much sugar causes me to crash 16-20 miles into a long run the following day. And JT doesn't eat desserts.

We reckoned on needing 5000 to 5500 calories a day. We certainly never felt light on energy although we did lose approximately a stone each over the month. For JT this was probably a problem, for me, a huge blessing!

Daily menu (sample)

Breakfast
2 pieces of toast and honey
1 pint water
1 cup coffee

Running breaks
Peanut butter and jam or ham salad sandwich
Chocolate raisins
Crisps
Coffee/soup
1 pint water (to boost hydration)
Fruit bar
Banana

Post finish
Chips
Garlic bread
Fruit bar
Jelly babies/chocolate raisins

Evening meal
Stir fry
Pasta bake
Pasta and sauce
Steak
The occasional Cornish Pasty
All with lots of fresh vegetables and usually extra noodles

On the run
Alternated Luzozade sport and water
500ml per session

Maps & Navigation

OS Landranger maps - 1:50,000

11, 12, 17, 21, 26, 34, 41, 50, 56, 63, 64, 71, 78, 85, 86, 90, 97, 102, 108, 109, 117, 118, 126, 137, 149, 162, 172, 181, 182, 191, 192, 193, 200, 201, 203, 204.

I bought the majority of maps new in bulk, for a discount price, because they needed to be up-to-date. But I also bought two or three second-hand off e.bay because they only featured a small part of the route.

The route was also mapped on **www.mapmyrun.com** which we carried on the iPhone along with a daily route description which was printed out from this site (available when you sign up as a Gold member, you can upgrade for a single month.)

As a back up we also marked our route on the **AA Close-up Britain Road Atlas - the largest scale road atlas of Britain,** ISBN 978-0-7495-5806-2. Having marked the route with a highlighter and put yellow dots every 10 miles and a red dot for the thirty and orange for campsites I taped the pages so that one could move easily from one section to the next.

Another App that came in handy was **Maps.** It enabled us to know exactly where we were, and a dot moves with you so you can easily check if you have taken the correct turn. Another valuable use is plotting a route. By dropping a pin where you want to get to it highlights the route which you can then follow in real time.

If you want to find local cycle paths, Sustrans provide a free app: **National Cycle Network.** Again very useful for planning alternative routes when the road is too dangerous etc

A further app invaluable for day to day navigation is **Find Friends.** By having Greg as a friend (and vice-versa) I could always see where he was, live on a map. Very useful for locating the van, meeting up on route or for him to know how we were doing.

> To view, or use, our actual detailed route go to:
> **www.mapmyrun.com/routes/view/24843402**

Our major sponsors

HEXX

Hexx's very generous sponsorship probably saved our lives - literally. Through their HexxTalent programme, not only did they work extremely hard to produce and provide our specially designed hi-viz running vests complete with sponsorship details. They also offered us nutrition advice, training wear, a video blog opportunity and as if that wasn't enough they also gave us a donation to The Cure Parkinson's Trust, 10% of all sales from their Classic Hoodies and HexxTexx sales for the period we were running. Huge thanks to Henry, Natalie, Jack and Graham. We are Hexxtraordinarily grateful.

hexx.co.uk

RAM Tracking

James Taylor's terrific piece of kit enabled friends, family and sponsors to follow our progress, minute by minute as a blue spot on a Google map. James not only provided the kit but also set up a personalised event website for us that along with the map linked directly to our Virginmoneygiving site. It was a terrific addition to our blog and publicity and enabled us to raise our profile and thus our fundraising even higher. Thank you James, especially for all the hard work sorting out the early teething problems. We really, really appreciated all that you did for us. Where would we have been without you?

ramtracking.com

Branded Promotional Products

You would never have thought that of all the kit required to run from one end of the country to the other the hardest item to find was a red beach ball! I searched everywhere, including the internet, but with no joy. Eventually I came across Branded Promotional Products who advertised packs of 100! In desperation, I rather cheekily contacted John Wray (the MD) and he came up trumps, and refused to charge me anything. Thank you John for your generosity, without you we wouldn't have been able to finish!

promotional-product.co.uk

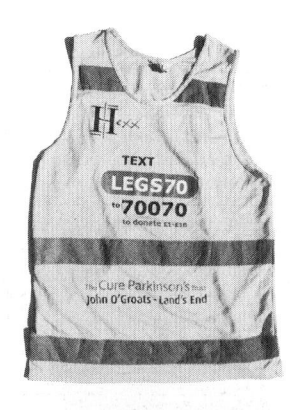

We didn't actively seek out companies to help us. Finding it hard to believe that anyone would want to align themselves with such an absurd venture. But these guys went above and beyond in their support and enabled us to achieve not only our goal but our fundraising target as well.

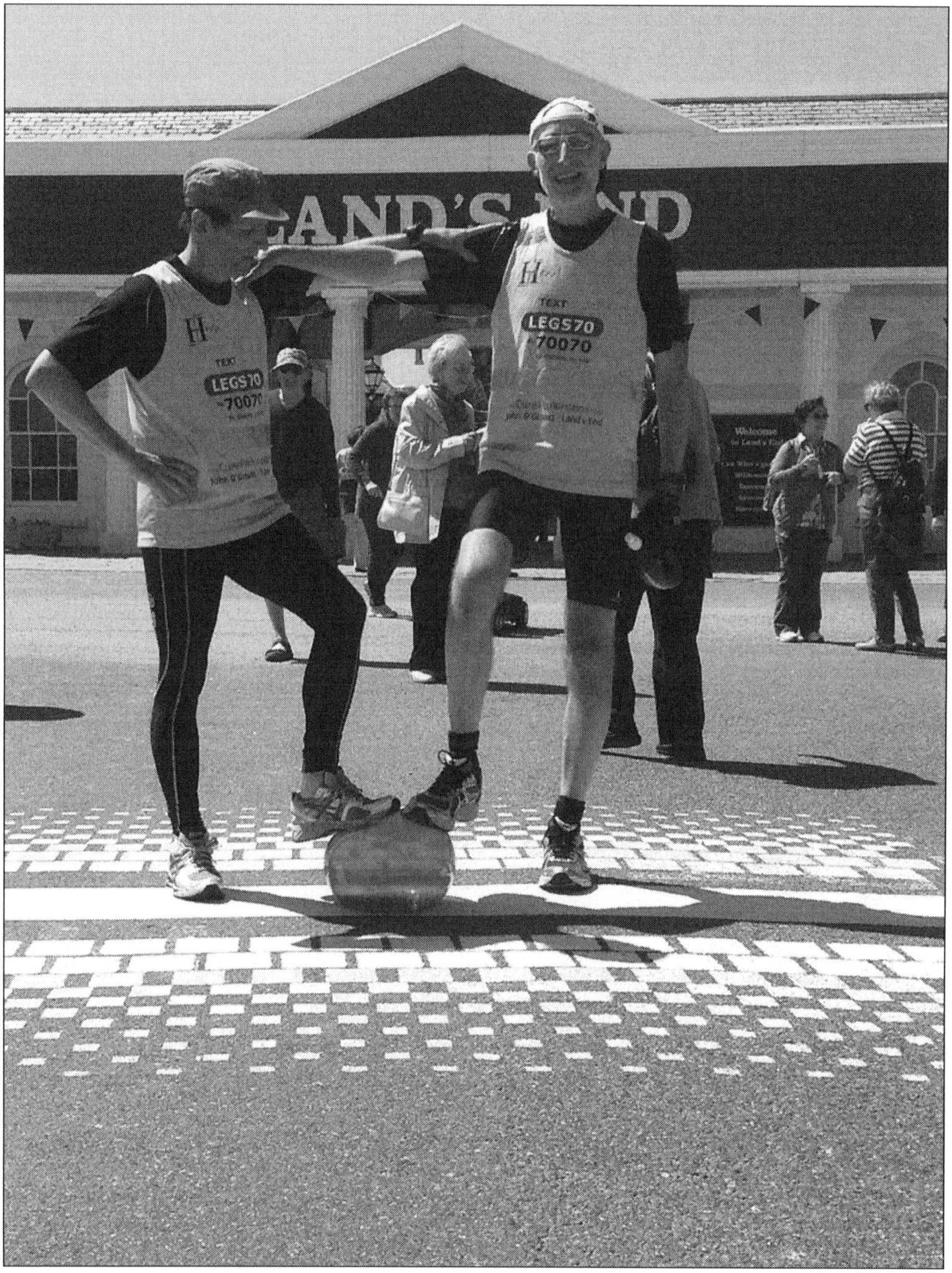
LAND'S
TEXT
LEGS70
70070
Welcome

'I hitch-hiked round Ireland with a fridge. John and Peter are running the length of Britain in under a month. The similarities are there for all to see, except for the fact that I was driven everywhere in cars, and then strolling into pubs, and they'll be running everywhere and then collapsing into exhausted heaps at the end of every day. All the more reason for supporting them - not least because their endeavours are all about finding a cure for Parkinson's. And, fridge or not, that's the coolest thing of all'

Tony Hawks

On route to find a cure...
Mon 23rd April - Mon 21st May 2012

Please support John & Peter on their run from John O'Groats to Land's End in aid of The Cure Parkinson's Trust

For more information or to follow their progress live please visit their blog: **www.offexploring.com/jogler**
Or find them on Twitter: **@TheJogler**
Or to sponsor them on line please go to:
www.virginmoneygiving.com/team/TheJogleBrothers
or text **LEGS70** to **70070** for free to donate £1-£10

If you feel inspired to make a donation to The Cure Parkinson's Trust please visit:

www.cureparkinsons.org.uk/Appeal/donate-now

Or for more information about The Cure Parkinson's Trust please visit their website:

www.cureparkinsons.org.uk

Thank you - *Peter & John, The Jogle Brothers*

The Cure Parkinson's Trust
Charity Number: 1111816

The End

...or is it?